The Division of Europe after World War II: 1946

W. W. Rostow
The Division of Europe after World War II: 1946

<svg>⬦</svg> University of Texas Press, Austin

First Edition, 1981

Requests for permission to reproduce material from this work
should be sent to
Permissions, University of Texas Press
Box 7819
Austin, Texas 78712

Library of Congress Cataloging in Publication Data

Rostow, W. W. (Walt Whitman), 1916–
    The division of Europe after World War II: 1946
    (Ideas and action series)
    1. World War, 1939–1945—Peace.   2. Europe—Politics and
government—1945–   3. Reconstruction (1939–1951)—
Europe.   4. United States—Foreign relations—1945–1953.
I. Title.   II. Series.
D816.R67   940.55′4   81-11640
                        AACR2
ISBN 0-292-70358-9
ISBN 0-292-70359-7 (pbk.)

To Charles Poor Kindleberger

Contents

Tables

Preface

This is the second in a series of essays centered on the relationship between ideas and action. The first was *Pre-Invasion Bombing Strategy: General Eisenhower's Decision of March 25, 1944.* Here we are in the world of diplomacy focusing on a decision which, I believe, helps illuminate the process by which the Cold War came about.

As for the general theme of the series, I would define ideas as the abstract concepts in the minds of public officials and their advisers which they bring to bear in making decisions. My experiences as both an academic and a public servant have equally driven home over the years this piece of wisdom from George Santayana's *Character and Opinion in the United States:*

> . . . human discourse is intrinsically addressed not to natural existing things but to ideal essences, poetic or logical terms which thought may define and play with. When fortune or necessity diverts our attention from this congenial ideal sport to crude facts and pressing issues, we turn our frail poetic ideas into symbols for those terrible irruptive things. In that paper money of our own stamping, the legal tender of the mind, we are obliged to reckon all the movements and values of the world.

But there is, of course, a good deal more to decisions in public policy than clash and choice among the "frail poetic ideas" we create to make simplified sense of an inordinately complex and usually disheveled field of action. A decision is, after all, a choice among perceived alternatives. Ideas play a large role in defining those alternatives, but the choice among them involves other factors. The precise setting and timing of the decision evidently matter. So do questions of power, that is, politics and bureaucratic vested interests. So do personalities—unique human beings, controlled by memories and experiences, dreams and hopes which James Gould Cozzens evoked, in *By Love Possessed*, in a definition of temperament:

> A man's temperament might, perhaps, be defined as the mode or modes of a man's feeling, the struck balance of his ruling desires, the worked-out sum of his habitual predispositions. In themselves, these elements were inscrutable. There were usually too many of them; they were often of irreducible complexity; you could observe only results. . . . The to-be-observed result was a total way of life.

And, as we shall see in the story told here, temperaments thus broadly defined sometimes clash at both the working levels and the highest reaches of government, adding a special wild card to the way history unfolds.

In this effort to illuminate the relationship between ideas and action, I decided to proceed as follows. First, to examine a series of eight or nine specific decisions taken by particular high public officials at particular times and to reflect on the decision-making process as a whole in a final essay. In the case studies, the decision would be briefly described, including the options which the executive perceived as available to him; the conceptual debate involved in the decision—the more or less pure intellectual content of the process—would be delineated; the larger background of events would be evoked; the interplay between the conceptual debate and the other more mundane forces in play would be examined; the follow-on events and consequences of the decision would be weighed; and some larger lessons of the story would be drawn. Along the way an effort would be made to capture the odd, often adventitious circumstances which entered into the decision and into the way things actually turned out. There are strands of accident and even humor—high, low, or wry—running through a good many of these case studies as well as pratfalls from which even the highest officials are not exempt.

I have chosen to examine decisions in which I played some role or which I had an opportunity to observe closely at the time. But, as the reader will perceive, this and the other volumes in the series are not exercises in autobiography. It is simply the case that one has a better chance of capturing something of the relationship between ideas and the other elements determining action if one was reasonably close to events than if the whole complex setting has to be reconstructed from the beginning.

On the other hand, my memory of the circumstances, the material in my files, and my knowledge of some of the actors were patently inadequate. In this and the other case studies, my purpose is to bring to bear what public records, communication with participants, and the literature of published memoirs and works of scholarship can now provide. As in the present volume, there is usually a formidable body of relevant material available.

Certain source or other basic materials, hitherto unpublished or not easily accessible, have been assembled in the appendixes to this book. They are meant to illuminate facets of the decision examined or to capture something of the moods and temper of the time.

The first essay in this series was about a decision well documented and with an established place in the standard histories of air power during the Second World War. This volume focuses on a much more obscure decision, only occasionally referred to in studies of the period. But I do believe that, as we track through this story, the coming of the Cold

War emerges as the result of a process somewhat different from that incorporated in either orthodox or revisionist versions of post-1945 diplomatic history. I would also note here an observation made in the final chapter of this book: if, as seems wholly possible, the abiding nationalism and rising desire for human freedom in Eastern Europe yield in the times ahead a crisis beyond the Soviet capacity to manage, the West may yet have to offer something like the Acheson-Clayton proposal as an alternative to cataclysm.

Dr. Ted Carpenter, a scholar of this period, has been of invaluable assistance both in mobilizing relevant primary and secondary sources and as a critic of drafts. Our work on this essay was supported by a grant from the University Research Institute of the University of Texas at Austin, whose indispensable help I wish warmly to acknowledge.

I should also like to thank the participants in these events and the scholars who have given their time for guidance and criticism: Joseph Alsop, Robert Asher, Harlan Cleveland, Harold van Buren Cleveland, Clark Clifford, Benjamin V. Cohen, Emilio Collado, Robert Divine, John Lewis Gaddis, John Kenneth Galbraith, Theodore Geiger, George Kennan, Charles P. Kindleberger, Václav Kostelecký, Clarence Lasby, Frederick Nolting, Paul R. Porter, Elspeth D. Rostow, Eugene V. Rostow, and Harrison Wagner.

As on many other occasions, I was aided in multiple ways by Lois Nivens. Frances Knape was most helpful in typing the various drafts.

I should add that this series of essays would not have been undertaken without the strong encouragement of my wife, Elspeth Davies Rostow, who believed I might usefully reflect on the large central question embedded in those periods in my professional life when I was diverted from strictly academic pursuits.

W. W. Rostow

July 1981
Austin, Texas

The Division of Europe after World War II: 1946

1. The Issue and the Decision

The decision which provided the focus for the first book in this series is a well-documented, even famous, event in military history, concerned as it was with the use of air power before D-Day. The minutes of the decisive meeting are available as well as accounts by a good many historians and, indeed, by two major participants. The decision which constitutes the point of departure for this essay took place in the wake of a meeting which leaves only faint tracks in the documentary record and only slightly more substantial reflections beyond.[1]

Nevertheless, the issue discussed at the meeting was, perhaps, the greatest of the post—World War II foreign policy questions. It may be that this was the only occasion during 1946 when the issue as a whole was explicitly addressed at a high level with lucid alternatives on the table; the timing was propitious; the participants (with an exception that will emerge) were of appropriate stature and responsibility; and an element in the proposal considered and initially rejected later came to life.

The participants were Secretary of State James Byrnes, Undersecretary Dean Acheson, and Assistant Secretary for Economic Affairs Will Clayton. The meeting probably took place on Saturday, April 20, 1946, shortly before Byrnes left for Paris to participate in treaty negotiations conducted by the

Council of Foreign Ministers scheduled to begin on April 25. The negotiations included the treaties for Finland, Bulgaria, Rumania, Hungary, and Italy but excluded Germany and Austria, which were, for the time, set aside after abortive efforts by Byrnes to bring them under consideration. Their affairs lay mainly in the hands of quadripartite Allied Control Councils in Berlin and Vienna.

The issue laid before Byrnes by Acheson and Clayton was the following: should the negotiation of the peace treaties in Europe, including Germany and Austria, be pursued separately, or should they be approached within the framework of a general settlement agreed on before the details of the treaties were negotiated?

We can assume that Acheson and Clayton argued along the following lines: strong forces were operating to bring about a split of Europe along the Elbe; the negotiation of the treaties, one by one, as existing procedures dictated, was likely to consolidate the split rather than prevent it; a similar potentially divisive process was at work in the Control Council negotiations in Berlin; before accepting this outcome and all it implied for Europe and the United States over the years ahead, a major effort should be made by the United States to reverse the course events appeared to be taking. To this end Acheson and Clayton, backed in the wings by Jean Monnet, laid before Byrnes a quite detailed plan. The rationale for that plan and its text in successive revisions are given in Appendix A. The plan had these elements:

1. The secretary of state would open the Paris meetings, scheduled to begin on the following Thursday, by taking a general initiative covering the whole range of unsettled European issues.

2. He would assert that the United States opposed the formation of exclusive blocs and the split of Europe they would bring about; that, whatever the outcome of his proposals, the American concern with the future of Europe was permanent

and not transient; and that the United States was prepared forthwith to make proposals for a European settlement on an all-European basis consistent with the wartime agreements.

3. He would propose formulas consistent with such a general European settlement, covering specific issues involved in the treaty negotiations (for example, the control of the Danube) and major issues outside the area of treaty negotiations, notably the major unsettled issues in Germany and Austria.

4. He would propose the setting up of a regional United Nations security council to oversee the execution of the settlements arrived at in the treaties as well as in Germany and Austria.

5. He would propose the creation of an all-European economic organization designed to accelerate lagging reconstruction and to achieve greater long-run economic unity in Europe, with subcommissions for fuel and power, trade and transport, finance, the coordination of plans, and so on.

6. He would assert, finally, that, should the settlement prove acceptable, the United States government would back the new economic organization of Europe with substantial economic aid.

Behind the plan was a central concern: the split of Europe was being accelerated by the judgment of Soviet, British, and French officials that the interest of the United States in the structure of Europe was likely to prove transitory, and, therefore, the Soviet Union had merely to await the progressive withdrawal of the United States before consolidating an Eastern European base and exerting pressure on the West; while the Western Europeans increasingly felt that the best they might look forward to was holding on to the area up to the Elbe and, perhaps, forming a western bloc. In effect, those supporting the plan felt that it was essential to reverse the impression left on Stalin and Churchill by Roosevelt's statement during the first session at Yalta—namely, that the United

States would not keep a large army in Europe and its occupation of Germany could be envisaged for only two years.[2] Subsequent U.S. behavior, in many ways evocative of 1919 to 1920, appeared to be validating that prediction, as old currents of isolationism reemerged.

The Acheson-Clayton proposal looked also to the longer run. It reflected the judgment that, if Germany were ever to be united, the legitimate fears of France and the smaller countries of Europe could be allayed only if the whole continent of Europe were so organized that the preponderant economic and political bargaining weight of a united Germany could not be wielded against the lesser European states. Moreover, the plan reflected the judgment of wise Europeans, including many Germans, who read the lesson of the two world wars as proof that the old European state system was no longer viable and that a united Europe was the proper objective for the creative energies of the postwar generation.

The proposal recognized that the Soviet Union had been proceeding in the post-Potsdam period on a unilateral basis in Europe and that the initiative proposed would cut clean across Stalin's apparent purposes. What then were the chances of success by negotiation with Moscow? The outcome was judged to depend on whether or not the Soviet performance was based on the assumption of future diminished American concern in European affairs. The argument explaining the proposal (see Appendix A) stated that:

> USSR response to the alternatives of a European Organization or vigorous US support for a Western bloc cannot fairly be pre-judged. . . . [It asserted, further, that the] nature of the alternative to a European Organization . . . makes it desirable in the U.S. interest to press for the superior solution, however small the chances of success may initially appear to be. Only after exhaustion of the line of approach it represents does acceptance of a bloc alternative appear justified.

The proposal did not deal explicitly with the question of political freedom in Eastern Europe, but one of its purposes was to provide a framework within which the natural East European orientation toward the West and aspiration for Western modes of political organization could become progressively more effective without endangering Soviet security, which would be provided for by the Soviet role in maintaining a disarmed, united democratic Germany. In the spring of 1946, Moscow had virtually consolidated Communist power in Bulgaria and Rumania; but, despite the role of Communists in key security posts, Czechoslovakia was still a politically democratic state, the Small Holders party had not yet been eliminated from power in Hungary, important democratic elements were still alive in Polish politics, and the shape of political life in the Soviet Zone of Germany had not been settled, despite Soviet efforts to enhance the influence of German Communists (see Appendix H). It was felt that the best chance for reversing the evident trend toward complete Soviet political and military consolidation of the area lay in a radical change in the shape which postwar negotiations were assuming—a change based on a credible United States initiative which would bring to bear "the full weight of its diplomatic power and bargaining position."

The concept had, in fact, been circulating and evolving in the State Department since February 25, 1946. For reasons explained below (pp. 53–62), I had drafted it while working in the State Department as assistant chief of the Division of German and Austrian Economic Affairs (GA), a division within the Office of Economic Security Policy (ESP). It made its way, with increasingly exalted bureaucratic support, to Clayton, within whose area my division fell. By an independent route it had also been made available to Acheson, with whom Clayton had evidently discussed it before taking it jointly to Byrnes. Because of its political as well as its economic content, I had, from the beginning, made the plan available to the political officers of the European Division (EUR), where it was, by and large, opposed. The plan itself and the controversy it generated in the State Department were reflected with some accuracy on April 24 and 25 in newspaper accounts (see Appendix B), whose authors had evidently checked widely in the State Department.[3]

Acheson and Clayton are reported in one case as "enthusiastic"; in another, Acheson, Clayton, and Byrnes' personal adviser Benjamin Cohen are characterized as in "at least partial support." James Dunn and H. Freeman Matthews, senior Foreign Service experts on Europe, are identified in one case as in "bitter opposition," in another as "major opponents." Byrnes is described as "interested" and as taking the plan to Paris for possible use, should a propitious occasion arise. We shall consider later the reasons for this division of opinion.

As the newspaper accounts suggest, Byrnes did not reject the Acheson-Clayton proposal out of hand. And in telegrams to Byrnes of May 9 (see Appendix C), at a critical moment in the Berlin Control Council negotiations, Acheson and Hilldring refer again to the danger of a definitive division of Germany and Europe, the need to forestall it if possible, and the possible evocation, among other measures, of "the plan submitted to you prior to your departure."[4] But, in fact, Byrnes did reject the plan by pocket veto. He proceeded with the treaty negotiations one by one, in effect trading to Moscow essentially what it wanted in the East for Trieste and Western interests in the Italian treaty negotiations, leaving Germany and Austria for later resolution. In September 1946 Byrnes offered, without avail, a long-term treaty to demilitarize Germany, a proposal he already had in mind at the April meeting. The Finnish, Bulgarian, Rumanian, Hungarian, and Italian treaties were finally agreed upon by the end of 1946 at sessions in New York. The outcome of the whole process was the consolidation in 1947 to 1948 of Communist rule in Poland, Czechoslovakia, and Hungary; a progressively formalized division of Germany with its regions ultimately integrated into NATO and the Warsaw Pact; a neutralized but democratic Finland; and, after laborious negotiations, the achievement in 1955 of a surprisingly benign settlement for Austria.

2. The Setting: 1946, a "Disastrous Year"

The setting in which Eisenhower's decision of March 25, 1944, was made was quite straightforward and, in a sense, simple: the invasion of the Continent was scheduled for late May or early June, and the Allied bombing forces evidently had a preparatory role to play. The question was what that role should be.

The setting of Byrnes' meeting of April 20, 1946, was much more complex. It occurred against the background of dynamic, interacting processes at work in Eastern Europe, Western Europe, the occupation of Germany and Austria, the peace treaty negotiations, and American politics. In fact, the conceptual debate among Americans on an appropriate approach to negotiations with the Soviet Union in 1946 cannot be understood outside the context of what was going on at home.

In a chapter heading of his book on Truman, Robert J. Donovan calls 1946 a "Disastrous Year." The description is apt. Released from the disciplines of war, the American people turned inward, in a manner evocative of 1919 and 1920, to pursue private and material goals. Under intense (but not universal) popular pressure, including demonstrations by men in the services, the armed forces were hastily dismantled, dropping from 11.4 million in 1945 to 3.4 million in 1946 and 1.6 million in 1947.[5] National defense expenditures on goods and services fell from $87 billion in 1945 to $19 billion in 1946, from 41 percent to 9 percent of the GNP. More important, the reductions in forces and expenditures left many military units essentially nonoperational, lacking key technical personnel. By March 1946 the army was down to 400,000 men, mainly new recruits. Price controls were substantially but not wholly abandoned, yielding a 16 percent inflation rate. Expenditures on durable consumer goods, constrained during the war years, almost doubled (in constant prices). But the surge of inflation had a sharp impact on real wages, which declined about 10 percent in 1946. This led to a series of acrimonious strikes for higher money wages, which generated a popular wave of hostility toward the unions. Starting with the interim report from Ottawa of a royal commission, which revealed a massive Soviet espionage effort in Canada, the issue of Soviet recruitment of American public servants was raised, an issue that was to haunt American politics for a decade. Within the Democratic party Truman's support eroded in both conservative southern and liberal northern camps. In late June Congress passed a bill weakening price controls in general and providing that price controls on meat could be reimposed only after August 20. When controls were, in fact, reimposed, cattle producers held their herds on the farm in a de facto strike, forcing a beef shortage. On October 14 Truman was forced to lift all price controls on agricultural products, but politically it was too late.

Thus, domestic political life turned very lively, indeed, in 1946. The Gallup poll registering presidential approval fell from 87 percent in July 1945 to 32 percent in October 1946. On November 6, 1946, the Republicans won their first congressional majority in both houses in fifteen years in what is often called the Beefsteak Election.[6] In its wake, Truman was almost universally judged to be a lame-duck president, to be superseded by a Republican in January 1949.

All this dishevelment, plain for all to see, within a nation which had emerged by V-J Day in a position of greater primacy even than Britain's after the Napoleonic Wars, had its impact throughout the world community and on the minds of those who bore responsibility for American foreign policy. In his famous X article, published in the July 1947 issue of *Foreign Affairs*, George Kennan evokes, in terms relevant to other periods since 1945 as well, its impact on the Communist world:

> . . . exhibitions of indecision, disunity and internal disintegration within this country have an exhilarating effect on the whole Communist movement. At each evidence of these tendencies, a thrill of hope and excitement goes through the Communist world; a new jauntiness can be noted in the Moscow tread; new groups of foreign supporters climb on to what they can only view as the band wagon of international politics; and Russian pressure increases all along the line in international affairs.[7]

Kennan's proposition was clearly at work during 1946 in every dimension of Soviet policy toward Europe, although, simultaneously, American public opinion was rapidly hardening in its view of Soviet policies and intentions (see below, pp. 83–84).

In Eastern Europe, however, Soviet policy faced a dilemma. On the one hand, the disposition of its armies in 1945 provided unlimited de facto power to do politically what the Soviet government wished to do. On the other hand, under the exigencies of war and wartime diplomacy, Stalin had made serious commitments to free secret elections in Eastern Europe in general, Poland in particular. After all, Britain had gone to war in defense of Poland, and, as Roosevelt made clear, there was a strong political interest in Poland's future in American political life. Poland was an obsessive subject of discussion and negotiation at Yalta. Churchill reports: "Poland was discussed at no fewer than seven of the eight plenary meetings of the Yalta Conference, and the British record contains an interchange on this topic of nearly eighteen thousand words between Stalin, Roosevelt, and myself."[8] Stalin was evidently resistant, seeking to maximize the power of the Polish Communists initially installed, but he gave ground under pressure from the United States and Britain.

Since this is a book about ideas and action, it is worth asking—rather than taking for granted—what Stalin had in mind. It so happens that a quarter century earlier, in a letter to Lenin, he had addressed himself in abstract terms to the question of how Communist states in Eastern Europe, assuming they emerged, should relate to the Soviet Union:

> For the nations constituting the old Russia, our (Soviet) type of federation can and must be regarded as of the greatest assistance on the road towards international unity. The reasons are obvious: these national groups either had no state organization in the past or had long ago lost it, so that the Soviet (centralized) type of federation could be grafted on without any special friction.
>
> The same cannot be said of those national groups not included in the old Russia as independent formations but having developed a specific state organization of their own, and which, if they become Soviet, will perforce have to enter into some State relation with Soviet Russia. Take for instance a future Soviet Germany, Poland, Hungary or Finland. It is doubtful whether these nations, who have their own State, their own army, their own finances, would, after becoming Soviet, at once agree to enter into a federal relationship with Soviet Russia of the Bashkir or Ukrainian type . . . they would regard federation of the Soviet type as a form of reducing their national independence and as an attempt against it.
>
> I do not doubt that the most acceptable form of rapprochement to these nationalities would be confederation. . . . I am leaving out the backward nationalities, e.g. Persia, Turkey, in relation to whom or for whom the Soviet type of federation and federation in general would be still more unacceptable.
>
> Bearing all this in mind, I think that it is indispensable to

include at some point in your minutes on the transition forms of rapprochement between the workers of the various nations the mention of *confederation* (alongside federation). Such an amendment would lend your proposals more elasticity, enrich them with one more transition form of rapprochement as described, and would render State rapprochement with the Soviet easier to the national groups which did not previously form part of old Russia.[9]

It would be quite unwarranted to assume that Stalin simply decided, as a matter of fixed plan, to implement after 1945 the "confederation" concept he commended to Lenin in 1920. A more general notion probably governed Soviet thought in the immediate postwar period. Built into the memory and doctrines of the Soviet leaders was an acute awareness that societies emerging from the political and social as well as the physical disruptions of major war represented targets of great opportunity. After all, it was by exploiting such possibilities that they had come to power in Russia in 1918, and it had been a close thing elsewhere in Central and Eastern Europe. From their perspective they no doubt felt a sense of historic duty to make the most of immediate postwar circumstances and extend Communism to the outer limits of the possible, short of direct military conflict with the United States. Their ambition was not limited to the areas controlled by the Soviet armies. The potentialities in France and Italy, western Germany, Greece, Turkey, and Iran evidently interested them. Stalin, whose style included elements of candor as well as guile, may have revealed his perspective quite succinctly in responding to Averell Harriman at Potsdam: "The first time I saw [Stalin] at the conference I went up to him and said that it must be very gratifying for him to be in Berlin, after all the struggle and tragedy. He hesitated a moment and then replied, 'Czar Alexander got to Paris.' It didn't need much of a clairvoyant to guess what was in his mind."[10] Stalin simply didn't know how far Moscow would be able to extend its power in the postwar world; but his ambitions were ample, supported by a sense of how much Russia had suffered and achieved in the Second World War, a determination to guarantee Soviet security from another German assault, converging with a Communist's sense of duty to exploit an interval of palpable opportunity.

As far as Eastern Europe was concerned, something like his confederation scheme, with ultimate power firmly centered in Moscow, was what emerged as the primary intent of the Soviet government. How far and how fast this could proceed, however, depended on the strength and determination of the United States in requiring that the Yalta commitments be carried out, notably with respect to Poland. In 1945 and subsequently, Stalin was not about to risk a confrontation which carried with it the risk of war with the United States. Nevertheless, Poland was critical from Moscow's point of view for fundamental reasons brought to public attention once again by the remarkable assertion of labor union independence in that country of 1980 and 1981. If Poland was taken over by more or less pliant Communists and became part of the confederation, a continuous area of military as well as political power could be built from Moscow as far west as the Elbe. If it were politically democratic, Poland might well be rendered harmless to the Soviet Union in narrow military terms, as Finland and Austria were to be; but it could not be relied on as a working member of a Moscow-dominated confederation. Eastern Germany, blocked off from the U.S.S.R. by a democratic Poland, would then be useful only as a diplomatic bargaining counter, in dealings with the West, to assure reparations or aid in the short run, the disarmament of a united democratic Germany in the long run.

Given their contrary visions of postwar Europe, Churchill and Roosevelt, on the one hand, and Stalin, on the other, were thus quite right to make Poland the central issue at Yalta. The final exchanges between the two Western leaders on the eve of Roosevelt's death reflect their anxiety about Stalin's evident procrastination in carrying out the Yalta agreement to broaden the government in Warsaw and to proceed with free elections; and this was the first major foreign policy issue addressed by Truman in his contentious meeting with Vyacheslav Molotov on April 23, 1945, followed by his dispatch of the ailing Harry Hopkins to Moscow a month later.

Hopkins got Stalin to agree that a Polish government of national unity be formed, including Stanislaw Mikolajczyk (a member of the wartime Polish government in London) as vice-premier. Three additional ministries were granted to non-Lublin Poles acceptable to Great Britain and the United States. With this and several lesser concessions, the ground was cleared for the Big Three meeting at Potsdam.

At Potsdam the recognition of the reorganized Polish Provisional Government was confirmed, and agreement was made to hold free and unfettered elections on the basis of universal suffrage and secret ballot, with guarantees of access to the world press to report events before and during the elections. In a sense, then, Truman's diplomacy on Poland in the first four months of his administration appeared to have moved the Polish question forward in terms of the Yalta agreement.

Mikolajczyk arrived in Warsaw as vice-premier to find the Communists quite solidly entrenched. The Ministry of the Interior was divided in two at the start, with public administration (routine bureaucratic matters) under Wladyslaw Kiernik, a follower of Mikolajczyk, and security (secret political police, internal security corps, and militia) under a Communist, Stanislaw Radkiewicz. What was left of the army was also controlled, at least at the top, by Communists and included many who had served in the Red Army. The third crucial position occupied by the Communists was the Ministry of Regained Territories (the Oder-Neisse region), a separate administration under Wladyslaw Gomulka. Since the territory was comparatively rich in industrial and agricultural opportunities, and since a complete resettlement of Poles from the East was called for after the Germans were expelled, ample possibilities for patronage and control were available to Gomulka, who was also at that time secretary of the Polish Communist party.

After Mikolajczyk's original Peasant party had been taken over by the Communists, two leaders of the new Polish Peasant party, which he then established, were murdered. Mikolajczyk's protests and demands for investigation were taken to exhibit a "lack of confidence in the Minister of Security." A subsequent trial brought a suitable confession from an underground agent.

Nevertheless, Mikolajczyk was able to hold a party congress in January 1946 and, despite harassment, maintained a distinctive political position. In the plebiscite of June 1946—conducted with many irregularities but more or less on Western election standards—the government announced, after a delay of ten days and much embarrassment, an antigovernment majority of 68 percent on the one disputed question (the abolition of the Senate); but according to Mikolajczyk the result would have been 83 percent in his favor had there not been arrests and falsification. It was Mikolajczyk who had urged the Polish people to vote "no" on this issue, which was universally taken to be a test of his strength.

From this time on, the Polish government, frightened by Mikolajczyk's evident grass-roots support, moved quickly under Moscow's guidance. To prepare for the parliamentary elections of January 1947, the western territories, safe under Gomulka's control, were given disproportionate electoral representation. Mikolajczyk and his followers were incriminated by the confessions of certain political prisoners who asserted they were foreign agents. Two bogus parties were set up to drain off the peasant vote toward Communist-controlled groups, thousands of members of the Polish Peasant party were at least temporarily arrested, and "voluntary open voting" took place in many districts. The resulting parliament, overwhelmingly backing the government bloc, passed a new provisional constitution in February 1947. Britain and the United States protested that the Yalta provisions on Poland were being violated, but by this time it was clear to both the Soviet leadership and the Polish Communists that such paper protests could be safely ignored.

This, in effect, was the end of the road for Yalta and Mikolajczyk; but he did not give up the uneven struggle and leave Poland until the fall of 1947, when he was informed of his imminent arrest. We shall consider later why this happened; but the fact is that, after Potsdam, the question of the fate of democracy in Poland virtually disappeared from Truman's and Byrnes' agenda.[11] The confrontation between Soviet and Western conceptions of postwar Europe shifted to Germany and the Control Council in Berlin.

The story of postwar policy toward Germany begins formally with the Potsdam meeting and its decisions, although a good deal was foreshadowed in the European Advisory Commission agreement on the location of occupation zones and the creation of a quadripartite Control Council in Berlin. As it related to Germany, the Potsdam communiqué issued on August 2, 1945, contained several elements. In part, it proclaimed general principles which were to govern the occupation of each zone in Germany. The principles were to be interpreted and administered by the several occupying powers; but the four-power Control Council in Berlin was to handle all-German issues, and a Council of Foreign Ministers was created to deal, among other matters, with German issues not resolved in Berlin and ultimately with a German treaty. The principles covered the elimination of existing military equipment and uniquely military production facilities as well as the democratization of German institutions: the schools, the judiciary, local government, and the trade unions. The principles of freedom of speech and assembly and of free elections were proclaimed.

The second set of agreements on Germany related to economic policy and, most specifically, to reparations; and it laid down a number of operating policies. Germany was to be treated as an economic unit, and central German agencies were to be created in economic fields, to operate under the Control Council. Germany was to pay reparations within the general limit of earning for itself a standard of subsistence accommodated to an average European level and within a specific limit of paying out of current exports for current imports. Soviet and Polish reparations were to come from the Soviet Zone; but, in view of heavy Russian war losses, 15 percent of Western Zone capital equipment removed would be traded against current exports from the Soviet Zone, and an additional 10 percent would be available as pure reparations to the Soviet Union. A general reparations plan was to be negotiated in the Control Council within six months. Advance reparation deliveries on a limited basis were to be made, pending a general accord, in order to accelerate European recovery.

Diplomatic explorations and technical studies of the reparations problem had been going forward since the Yalta conference, the negotiations being conducted on the American side mainly under a special group headed by Edwin Pauley. That group was ill coordinated with other arms of American foreign policy, and there was still no clear American position on reparations formulated at the time of the Potsdam conference.

At Potsdam, however, the American delegation underwent a vivid experience which clarified its collective mind. Americans saw in Berlin (including the Western zones of Berlin) that, without inter-Allied agreement, the Russians were moving equipment out of factories as fast as their technicians could dismantle it—faster even than the equipment could be properly crated and transported, and it was evident that this process of Soviet seizure was proceeding throughout much of Eastern Europe as well as in Manchuria. American reparations policy quickly focused around the problem of preventing the kind of denuding of West Germany which the Russians were effecting in the East.

Mindful of the Russian war losses, Americans found it hard in July 1945 to put their hearts into protesting what was being done in the Soviet Zone, even though the hasty unilateral removal of machinery was viewed as inefficient as well as illegal. American effort, therefore, was devoted primarily to limiting the extent of Soviet claims on West German capital equipment and to laying down rules under which it would be impossible for the United States to pour emergency aid into Germany from the West (or finance a German foreign exchange deficit) while current German production was being drained off to the East as reparations. Thus, while Potsdam's general political and economic principles looked to a united four-power policy in Germany, the unilateral principle was strengthened once unilateral action on reparations was accepted as legitimate in the Soviet Zone; and reparations went to the heart of short-run economic and political policy. To a significant degree, then, the postwar negotiations on German unity began on the basis of a split Germany.

From the Potsdam meetings to April 1946, the question of reparations remained the central issue of four-power diplomacy in Germany, although the larger issues emerged and were gradually clarified. On December 12, 1945, the Department of State issued a long statement on German economic policy. Its formal purpose was to clarify the principle on which the reparations clauses of Potsdam should be negotiated. Its broader aim, however, was to define the stages whereby the German economy would move from a role of subservience to the needs of other states to recovery and, finally, to resumed economic development when once again German standards of living would be a matter determined by German efforts and efficiency in utilizing German resources. This document symbolized the rapid transition in the post-Potsdam period from a negative to a constructive approach to Germany, a transition which was inevitable given Western values but which was certainly accelerated by a Soviet policy which evidently sought to profit from poverty and frustration in Central and Western Europe.

Although the economists and industrial technicians concentrated in Berlin made valiant efforts to construct an economic plan which would meet the complex Potsdam conditions, the essence of American policy in this period was political. The American purpose was to force at an early stage a clear-cut test of whether or not the Soviet Union was prepared to move promptly toward a united Germany. The architect of this policy, as well as its chief practitioner, was Lucius Clay.

The reparations plan was essentially a definition of the initial complement of industrial equipment necessary to make postwar Germany economically viable if it were effectively unified. The reparations pool would be defined by subtracting this minimum level of industry from the capacity actually in Germany. Clay's policy was to work hard and cooperatively with the Russians in getting an agreed level-of-industry plan for Germany as a whole and then to make actual reparation deliveries hinge on Soviet agreement to treat the German economy as an economic unit. Because of the intimate interconnections between economic and other institutions, it was clear that political and economic unity would come together if they came at all. What appeared a highly remote and often fantastic technicians' game was, in fact, a negotiation to test whether the split of Germany would persist.

The outcome was clean-cut, although its full implications took some time to absorb. A level-of-industry plan was agreed on March 26, 1946, with the American negotiators making every possible concession to meet Soviet demands. Within a month, however, Clay had openly disengaged from the reparations plan on the grounds that the Soviets were clearly unprepared to join in a common program for foreign trade and for the German economy as a whole. Clay's statement in the Coordinating Committee of the Control Council on April 26, 1946, reveals his mind:

> I submit that reparations was only one of the bricks that built the house. If you pull out any of the bricks the house collapses, and it seems to me we have pulled out so many already we are on the verge of collapse. I don't believe we can ever reach a solution on any one of them without reaching a solution on all of them. Certainly the question of the ability to meet the export-import program is tied up definitely with the question of reparations.
>
> Since it has become the practice to quote Potsdam, I would like to quote a part of Potsdam which comes before the part quoted by my Soviet colleague. Paragraph 14 requires that during the occupation Germany shall be treated as a single economic unit. During the year of occupation up to date, I would not think anyone can claim that we have done so. In Paragraph 15 it states that Allied control shall be imposed on the German economy only to the extent necessary to insure during the term of the Control Council the equitable distribution of essential commodities between the several zones, so as to produce a balanced economy throughout Germany, and reduce the need for imports. We have been here a year, but I do not believe that my colleagues would claim that we have accomplished that. And Paragraph 16 shows that the writers of this protocol foresaw what might happen and required to carry it out the establishment of German administrative machinery to proclaim and assume the administration of these controls. Would my colleagues suggest that we have lived up to this part of Potsdam? I claim that to live up to Potsdam you live up to it in whole and not in its individual parts.[12]

On May 3 Clay stopped advance reparation deliveries to the Soviet Union from the American Zone—a major bench mark in the evolution of postwar diplomacy.

Hopes for an all-German settlement were not immediately

and definitively abandoned; but, from this time forward, the American position moved toward the unification of the Western zones and the gradual acceptance of a split Germany. This trend was broken only by George C. Marshall's last-ditch effort to negotiate German unity in Moscow in March and April 1947 and, in a sense, by his offer in June 1947 to treat the whole of Europe as an economic unit under the Marshall Plan proposal.

It is difficult to recapture the mood of the post-Potsdam negotiations in the Berlin Control Council as American hopes came up against the Soviet, British, and French positions, each, for different reasons, not anxious to move toward German unity. Eisenhower and Clay—the former remaining in Germany only until November 1945—felt that the Control Council and its negotiations represented a historic occasion to seek a fundamental understanding with the Russians. Eisenhower articulated this view as follows:

> Obstacles, doubts, fears of failure in American-Soviet relations, there were on every side. But the alternative to success seemed so terrifying to contemplate that all of us on occupation duty sought every possible avenue through which progress might be achieved.
>
> Berlin, we were convinced, was an experimental laboratory for the development of international accord. There the West was joined with the East in the task of reorganizing a highly complex economy and re-educating a numerous people to political decency so that Germany, purged of its capacity and will for aggression, might be restored to the family of nations.
>
> If in that endeavor there could be developed friendly ways and means of solving our local differences and problems, a long step forward would be taken toward the friendly settlement of world problems. Overshadowing all goals for us Americans was the contribution we locally might make toward establishing a working partnership between the United States and Russia.[13]

From the beginning, Eisenhower was encouraged by the responsiveness of Georgi K. Zhukov; and between Clay and Vasily Sokolovsky, their deputies and successors, there developed a relationship of mutual respect and, to a degree, of friendship.[14] This reaching out between Americans and Russians, within the narrowing limits the course of events permitted, extended far down into the maze of technical committees into which the Control Council was organized. Although reparations was at the center of high diplomacy in Berlin, there was an interminable array of housekeeping questions which required one form or another of expertise. Neither the Americans nor the Russians involved in this business were professional diplomats. They were, for the most part, technicians, emerging from searching experiences of war, full of national pride, and touched with a human desire to make the peace work. The Berlin Control Council was the most extensive Western contact with the rising second generation of well-trained technicians in Soviet society; and many who shared the experience emerged with a sense that Soviet society had the capability of producing in time a policy easier to live with than Stalin's.

The Control Council quickly established a common law of decorous, dignified debate, a tradition which survived long after the council had clearly failed in its central mission. On at least one occasion Sokolovsky, furnished by the powerful Soviet political adviser with a conventional diplomatic script full of the increasingly conventional recriminations against the West, did his duty but in a manner that clearly disassociated him from the text. In part, the Control Council style was a carry-over of mutually understood military etiquette as among the military chiefs; in part, it reflected a sense of larger mission which, in differing degree, touched men from all of the four nations represented in Berlin.

This mood, of course, had little to do with policy. Policy on the Soviet side was determined in Moscow by Stalin. And at no point did Clay and his senior colleagues mistake the human warmth and willingness to compromise among their Russian colleagues for the substance of Soviet policy or Stalin's intent; at no point did they surrender American interests, as they were then understood, in order to get on with the Russians in some vague and general sense. Clay was clear that solid understanding and agreement could come only between self-respecting nations clear and firm concerning their essential interests.

The human relations which developed initially between the Americans and Russians in Berlin were watched with mixed feelings by the British and French. The rapprochement raised the possibility of a Soviet-American bilateral agreement which would, in effect, settle Europe's affairs and reduce all other powers to secondary status. More important, as far as the American hopes in the Control Council were concerned, neither the French nor the British believed then that German unity was a practical or a particularly desirable goal.

The French, having failed to get agreement on the detachment of the Ruhr, sought to delay the revival of German economic and political strength at every stage, sensing that a revived Germany would ultimately overshadow postwar France on the European scene. British policy, on narrower economic grounds, aimed to ensure a more rapid recovery of the British than the German economy, notably in export markets; but, since the costs of British occupation in Germany were high, there was a countervailing interest in making the British Zone, which contained the bulk of German industry, a going concern. Neither France nor Britain shared the American anxiety to force a showdown on the issue of German unity, both nations being reasonably content with the split of Europe on the Elbe as representing a tolerable, if not happy, distribution of power between East and West in the short run and, perhaps, in the long run as well. Given their recent experiences of Germany and their intense domestic preoccupations in the immediate postwar period, their attitudes were wholly understandable—but they were not in harmony with the more ambitious hopes and more ardent mood of Americans caught up in the German problem.

Some British and French undoubtedly shared the sense of promise implicit in the human understanding which briefly flowered in the Control Council. On the whole, however, Clay, in actively seeking an accord with the Russians on the level of industry and then provoking a sharp crisis on the issue of German economic unity, was doubly out of step with his Western colleagues.

Early in 1946 it became evident that Stalin was disturbed at the developing relationship in Berlin, which indeed had within it the seeds of German unity on democratic terms. There were changes in Soviet personnel, and the role of Soviet political adviser was increased. Zhukov was recalled as early as November 1945 and soon isolated in Odessa. Sokolovsky operated with progressively diminished flexibility and freedom for independent action.

After the failure of the reparations negotiation in April, the notion of linking the British and American zones began seriously to be considered. On July 20, 1946, a formal offer was made in the Control Council to link the American Zone with any other (or all three), and this was accepted by the British on July 30. Aside from aiding German recovery and strengthening the Western bargaining hand vis-à-vis Moscow, the agreement lifted to a degree the pressing financial burden of occupation on London and gave Clay a strong voice in the administration of West German resources, including the critical supply of coking coal from the Ruhr. It had rankled among the Americans in Berlin that their authority extended directly only over the wooded hills and farms which mainly characterized the American Zone in the south.

The American position taken in the Control Council shared one general limitation of American policy. It sought to test Soviet intentions at a key point, but it incorporated no clear, positive concept of Europe or of the American interest in its structure. German unity was sought in a vacuum, as a goal in itself or as a generalized test of Soviet intentions. Above all, the American view failed to recognize adequately the forces shaping Soviet policy and the extent to which Soviet policy hinged on what Stalin thought the United States would or would not do to enforce agreements he intended to break if violation proved safe.

The American assumption in the Control Council was that Moscow's position was determined by forces essentially independent of the American performance outside Berlin and that the maximum course open to the United States, having honestly reassured the Soviets that the nation's intentions were peaceful, was to accept the split on the Elbe.[15] The reaction in Berlin to the Acheson-Clayton proposal for an American initiative looking to an all-European settlement was that the question of unity or schism in Europe would be settled in Germany—and in Berlin. If the Soviets were willing to see a free unified Europe, that fact would emerge in the German negotiations; if not, then a split on the Elbe would be inevitable. There was little awareness that the fate of Germany might hinge on Mikolajczyk's fate in Poland and on what the United States did or failed to do in backing the Yalta and Potsdam commitments in Eastern Europe. And, in other respects as well, American policy in postwar Germany was clear, strong, but narrow.

Clay's performance in the eight post-Potsdam months had one important consequence for those charged with making American policy. His effort to seek German unity by negotiation with Russia had been so wholehearted and was conducted with such evident sincerity, and the Soviet unwillingness to proceed seriously toward unity was so patent, that no one who knew the circumstances could feel that a postwar opportunity for accord had been lost for lack of trying in Berlin.

As Stalin progressively consolidated his position in Eastern Europe and the Control Council in Berlin moved into stalemate and the de facto acceptance of the split of Germany,

Byrnes and his staff worked their way laboriously through the peace treaties. It was clear at the time to those working from day to day in the State Department and it is clear from Byrnes' account in *Speaking Frankly* that, at a crucial juncture in world history, the American secretary of state was overwhelmingly preoccupied with what were geographical and, in substance, peripheral issues. The relevant chapter headings of Byrnes' book suggest rather well the story of his treaty-making peregrinations over the critical sixteen months from September 1945 through December 1946: "Setback at London," "Moscow Ends an Impasse," "London Again, and Paris Twice," "The Paris Peace Conference and Its New York Finale." Of his 562 days as secretary of state, Byrnes spent 245 outside the United States, 350 away from Washington.

In all conscience, the negotiation of the treaties was hard and frustrating work, marked at every step by the skillful, patient, stubborn roadblocks and obfuscations for which Molotov was justly famous. The Council of Foreign Ministers was a very difficult committee. At the end, one can understand Byrnes' pride and relief that the job was done. And it was a job that had to be done. It brought Finland and Italy, as well as the other states, formally back into the family of nations. Byrnes took great pains to carry with him the leaders of the Senate in both parties. And on June 5, 1947, the politically most difficult of the treaties—the Italian—cleared the Senate. But, as they emerged, the treaties merely tidied up one dimension of the division of Europe.

Byrnes was by no means cut off from a role in other dimensions of foreign policy. His Stuttgart speech of September 6, 1946, was carefully prepared with the support of Senators Connally and Vandenberg and an important intervention by General Clay.[16] It not only offered the disarmament for forty years of a united Germany but also asserted the determination of the United States to maintain a long-term interest and involvement in Germany and Europe. It held up, as well, a vision of German movement toward self-government and finding "an honorable place among the free and peace-loving nations of the world." All this reflected authentic trends in U.S. policy by the end of the summer of 1946. There was also in the Stuttgart speech an element of response to the Soviet posture of appealing (and permitting the German Communists to appeal) to German nationalism and the aspiration for unity. But the fact is that, once committed to the treaty negotiations which proceeded in a series of floating crap games from one capital to another, Byrnes had little time to stand back and contemplate the larger process of progressive division at work and focus hard and in a sustained way on whether anything could be done to produce a better outcome. In Acheson and Clayton, Byrnes had exceedingly able deputies operating steadily in Washington. But the position of the secretary of state is—or should be—rather different from, say, that of Molotov. Molotov was an instrument of the policy agreed in Stalin's Politburo. The secretary of state is—or should be—the principal and most intimate collaborator of the president in the making of foreign policy. Byrnes' preoccupation with the treaties in 1946, combined, as we shall see, with his rather peculiar relation to Truman, permitted the process of division to go forward—in Eastern Europe, Berlin, and the treaty negotiations themselves—without any coherent, determined effort to reverse it.

These rather depressing developments in the world of politics and diplomacy took place against a background of uneven and financially precarious economic revival in Europe, reflected in Tables 1 to 5. The main features of the situation were these:

Industrial production, except for Germany, revived moderately well but declined or decelerated in the extremely severe European winter of 1946–47. Overall it remained below the 1938 level (Table 1).

Agricultural production, recovering more slowly, was far below the 1938 level (Table 2).

Sustained by ad hoc pre–Marshall Plan credits, European

TABLE 1. The Level of Industrial Production[a] in European Countries
(*Index numbers—1938 = 100*)

Country	Percentage of 1938 Total European Production[b]	1946				1947		
		First Quarter	Second Quarter	Third Quarter	Fourth Quarter	First Quarter	Second Quarter	Third Quarter
Belgium	3.24	77	85	93	99	99	106	102
Bulgaria	0.33	95	109	139	134	105	135	149
Czechoslovakia	3.39	70	70	83	87	96	101	93
Denmark	1.61	93	86	97	100	99	100	108
Finland	1.22	65	64	72	79	86	81	81
France	10.80	75	88	82	94	95	104	96
Germany (3 Western zones)	16.62	22	26	31	31	24	33	37
Greece[c]	0.75	44	55	61	67	64	71	71
Ireland	0.41	103	112	107	114	104	110	113
Italy	7.24	34	55	65	61	49	65	76
Netherlands	3.12	62	68	76	83	81	88	91

Norway	0.94	93	103	95	110	113	119	106
Poland	2.53	71	77	80	90	93	100	104
Sweden	3.56	101	100	102	104	101	100	103
United Kingdom	21.62	101	102	100	115	103	110	109
Total of above countries								
Including Germany	77.38	68	74	76	83	78	85	86
Excluding Germany	60.76	80	87	88	98	93	100	99

Note: The index numbers for each country (with the exception of the United Kingdom) have been taken from official or semiofficial sources. Where the original base of the index numbers was other than 1938, the figures have been adjusted to that base year by means of the official prewar index numbers. Adjustments have also been made, where necessary, to include building activities.

The weights used in arriving at the combined index numbers, shown at the bottom of the table, are roughly proportional to the net value of industrial production (including manufacturing, handicrafts, mining, and building) in 1938, expressed in U.S. dollars of 1938 purchasing power.

^aIncluding manufacturing, mining, and building.

[a]Including manufacturing, mining, and building.
[b]Excluding U.S.S.R.
[c]Excluding mining.

Source for Tables 1–5: Economic Survey of Europe in 1948, Research and Planning Division, Economic Commission for Europe (Geneva: United Nations, 1948), pp. 3, 11, 31, 54, and 59, respectively.

TABLE 2. The Level of Agricultural Production in Europe[a]
(Index numbers—1935–1938 = 100)

Country	Percentage of Prewar Total European Production[a]	1945–46	1946–47
Austria	1.63	56	63
Belgium	2.09	58	72
Bulgaria	1.54	49	73
Czechoslovakia	3.75	56	73
Denmark	1.93	87	94
Finland	1.02	73	76
France	15.72	50	73
Germany (3 Western zones)	10.61	68	65
Greece	1.21	41	77
Hungary	2.45	54	55
Ireland	1.50	111[b]	108[b]
Italy	8.42	79	77
Netherlands	2.58	56	79
Norway	0.62	75	87
Poland	9.36	33[b]	45[b]

Portugal	0.91	80	95
Rumania	3.57	34[b]	57[b]
Spain	5.39	49[c]	92[c]
Sweden	2.08	98	103
Switzerland	1.38	90	87
Turkey	2.33	119[b]	119[b]
United Kingdom	5.89	106	106
Yugoslavia	3.42	50	57
Total of above countries			
Including Germany	89.40	63	75
Excluding Germany	78.79	62	76

Note: The index numbers for 1946–47 (except for Switzerland) have been taken from a study on European agriculture prepared by the Food and Agriculture Organization of the United Nations. They have for each country been derived from a calculation of the value of output at prewar prices. Index numbers for 1945–46 have been estimated by using rough calculations of the gross value of production in 1938 prices for major cereals and animal products in 1945–46 as compared to 1946–47. For Switzerland, the rough index number has been related to 1938.

The weights used in arriving at the European index are percentages of the net value of prewar total European agricultural output (excluding the U.S.S.R.) accounted for by each country, in 1934–1936, calculated in U.S. dollars of 1933 purchasing power.

The index numbers refer to crop years July 1945–June 1946 and July 1946–June 1947.

[a] Excluding U.S.S.R.
[b] Base of the index numbers: 1934–1938.
[c] Base of the index numbers: 1930–1934.

33

imports were reasonably high, exports low, and intra-European trade disastrously low, in substantial part due to the extremely low level of economic activity in Germany (Table 3).

The European balance of payments deficits were much greater than in 1938 (as well as after the First World War), due not only to the trade deficit but also to lesser earnings from investments and invisibles (Tables 4 and 5). The balance of payments deficit came to rest on the need for enormous imports from the United States in foodstuffs, coal, and manufactured goods which could not be paid for by exports to the United States.

This situation, heightened by the hard winter of 1946–47, translated itself into mass impoverishment in Germany, straitened circumstances in varying degree elsewhere, and a generally disheartening setting for social and political life. Clearly something had to be done about the European dollar deficit and the revival of German economic life in 1947, or Western Europe was headed for disaster.

These, then, were the corrosive forces operating, on the whole quietly, without dramatic crises, during the year 1946: at home, in Eastern Europe, in the Control Council in Berlin, and among the economies of Western Europe.

TABLE 3. Europe's Trade Measured in Constant Prices, 1938, 1946, and 1947[a]

Year	Trade with Non-European Countries		Intra-European Trade[b]		Total Trade of Europe		Distribution of Total	
	Millions of Dollars at 1938 Prices	Percent of 1938	Millions of Dollars at 1938 Prices	Percent of 1938	Millions of Dollars at 1938 Prices	Percent of 1938	Trade with Non-European Countries Percent	Intra-European Trade Percent
1938								
Imports, f.o.b.	5,820	100	6,960	100	12,780	100	45.5	54.5
Exports, f.o.b.	3,730	100	6,960	100	10,690	100	34.9	65.1
1946								
Imports, f.o.b.	5,350	91.9	3,150	45.3	8,500	66.5	62.9	37.1
Exports, f.o.b.	2,300	61.7	3,150	45.3	5,450	51.0	42.2	57.8
1947								
Imports, f.o.b.	6,200	106.5	3,900	56.0	10,100	79.0	61.4	38.6
Exports, f.o.b.	2,900	77.7	3,900	56.0	6,800	63.6	42.6	57.4

[a]Figures for 1947 are provisional estimates based, in some cases, on partial data for the year.
[b]Including U.S.S.R.

TABLE 4. Europe's Balance of Payments with the United States and with Other Non-European Countries, 1938, 1946, and 1947 (*Thousand millions of current dollars*)

	1938			1946			1947[a]		
	United States	Other Non-Europe	Total	United States	Other Non-Europe	Total	United States	Other Non-Europe	Total
Europe's imports, f.o.b.	1.3	4.5	5.8	4.4[b]	5.0	9.4	5.9[b]	7.1	13.0
Europe's exports, f.o.b.	0.6	3.1	3.7	0.9	3.4	4.3	0.9	5.2	6.1
Balance on trade account	−0.7	−1.4	−2.1	−3.5	−1.6	−5.1	−5.0	−1.9	−6.9
Income from investments (net)	+0.1	+1.3	+1.4	+0.1	+0.4	+0.5	+0.1	+0.3	+0.4
Other current transactions, including shipping, travel, cinema royalties, military expenditures, etc. (net)	+0.2	+0.5	+0.7	−0.8	−0.4	−1.2	−0.5	−0.5	−1.0
Balance on current account	−0.4	+0.4	—	−4.2	−1.6	−5.8	−5.4	−2.1	−7.5

[a] Figures for 1947 are provisional estimates based, in some cases, on partial data for the year.

[b] Includes rough estimate for shipment of foodstuffs and other commodities to Germany under the United States Army civilian supply program. In addition to the import figures shown in the table, European countries in 1946 and 1947 acquired considerably more than $1,000 million of goods, valued at depreciated sales price as distinguished from original cost, from United States war surplus stocks remaining in Europe at the end of the war. Most of these goods were acquired on a long-term credit basis.

TABLE 5. Europe's Balance of Payments with Non-European Countries after the First World War and Second World War (*Thousand millions of current dollars*)

	1919 and 1920[a]	1946 and 1947[a]
Europe's imports, f.o.b.	19.7	22.4
Europe's exports, f.o.b.	7.7	10.4
Balance on trade account	−12.0	−12.0
Income from investments (net)	+1.8	+0.9
Other current transactions (net)	+2.2	−2.2
Balance on current account	−8.0	−13.3

Note: Data for 1919 and 1920 are consolidated from separate balance of payments estimates for Continental Europe and for the United Kingdom, with imports and shipping adjusted from c.i.f. to f.o.b. basis and with all figures adjusted to eliminate transactions between Continental Europe and the United Kingdom.

[a] Figures are totals for twenty-four months' period in each case. The 1947 estimates included in these figures are provisional.

3. The Foreign Service Outlook on the Prospects for Europe

The debate on the plan laid before Byrnes by Acheson and Clayton on April 20, 1946, occurred in the midst of these dynamic processes but before they had yielded definitive results. At the working level the major partisans, as indicated earlier, were the members of the Foreign Service concerned with European affairs and the economists of the Office of German-Austrian Economic Affairs, in particular Charles Kindleberger, its chief, and myself. And by early 1946 the options were quite clear: a major purposeful U.S. effort to avoid the split of Europe or its acceptance.

The Foreign Service did not take a uniform position but, by and large, some of its most influential members had concluded in the course of 1945 or were coming to conclude in 1946 that a split of Germany and Europe on the Elbe was the most realistic and likely result of the forces at work. Since this view antedated the Acheson-Clayton proposal of 1946, it properly forms part of the background to it.

As the most formally intellectual member of the Foreign Service, George Kennan was one of the first to articulate the case for a split Europe. He wrote, from his post in Moscow, to Charles Bohlen stating the proposition rather starkly—a letter Bohlen received as he arrived for the Yalta conference on February 3, 1945. Here are Bohlen's quotations from and paraphrase of Kennan's letter:

"I am aware of the realities of this war, and of the fact that we were too weak to win it without Russian cooperation. I recognize that Russia's war effort has been masterful and effective and must, to a certain extent, find its reward at the expense of other peoples in eastern and central Europe.

"But with all of this, I fail to see why we must associate ourselves with this political program, so hostile to the interests of the Atlantic community as a whole, so dangerous to everything which we need to see preserved in Europe. Why could we not make a decent and definitive compromise with it—divide Europe frankly into spheres of influence—keep ourselves out of the Russian sphere and keep the Russians out of ours? That would have been the best thing we could do for ourselves and for our friends in Europe, and the most honest approach we could have tried to restore life, in the wake of war, on a dignified and stable foundation.

"Instead of this, what have we done? Although it was evident that the realities of the after-war were being shaped while the war was in progress we have consistently refused to make clear what our interests and our wishes were, in eastern and central Europe. We have refused to name any limit for Russian expansion and Russian responsibilities, thereby confusing the Russians and causing them constantly to wonder whether they are asking too little or whether it was some kind of a trap."

As an alternative program Kennan suggested, in addition to the "partition of Europe," the following:

1. That plans for the United Nations be buried "as quickly and quietly as possible," because the only practical effect of creating an international organization would be to commit the United States to defend a "swollen and unhealthy Russian sphere of power."

2. That the American people be corrected of the "dangerously erroneous impression that the security of the world depends on our assuming some formal blanket engagement to use our armed force in some given set of circumstances, as set forth in some legal documents." The United States must reserve to itself the right to decide where to use armed force.

3. That the United States should write off Eastern and Southeastern Europe unless it possessed the will "to go whole hog" and oppose with all its physical and diplomatic resources Russian domination of the area.

4. That the United States "accept as an accomplished fact the complete partition of Germany" and begin consultations with the British and French about the formation of a Western European federation, which would include West German states.

Bohlen's reply and reflections on the exchange capture well the balance of considerations that governed American policy at Yalta.

Because I was so busy, I could write only a hasty reply:

"I can't say I have given your letter the attention it deserves, but there is simply not time. As you know, there is a very great deal in your expositions that I agree with. You should know that in this connection the U.S. government is following admittedly a policy of no small risk. But have you ever seriously thought through the alternatives? The 'constructive' suggestions that you make are frankly naïve to a degree. They may well be the optimum from an abstract point of view. But as practical suggestions they are utterly impossible. Foreign policy of that kind cannot be made in a democracy. Only totalitarian states can make and carry out such policies. Furthermore, I don't for one minute believe that there has been any time in this war when we could seriously have done very differently than we did. It is easy to talk about instruments of pressure that we had in our hands. But the simple fact remains that if we wished to defeat Germany we could never have even tried to keep the Soviet armies out of Eastern Europe and Germany itself. I can never figure out why a piece of paper that you did not get should be regarded as so much more real than those you did get. Isn't it a question of realities and not of bits of paper? Either our pals intend to limit themselves or they don't. I submit, as the British say, that the answer is not yet clear. But what is clear is that the Soyuz [Soviet Union] is here to stay, as one of the major factors in the world. Quarreling with them would be so easy, but we can always come to that."

What I was saying so cryptically to Kennan was that, as usual, I agreed in general with his analysis of the situation, but I thought he was far off target in his conclusions. I recall feeling quite strongly that to abandon the United Nations would be an error of the first magnitude. While I had my doubts about the ability of a world organization to prevent big-power aggression, I felt that it could keep the United States involved in world affairs without, as Kennan thought, committing us to use force when we did not want to.

As for the partition of Germany, the domination of Eastern Europe by the Soviet Union, and the general idea of dividing the Continent into spheres of influence, I could not go along with Kennan. To me, acceptance of a Soviet sphere, instead of relieving us of responsibility, would compound the felony. Any formal, or even an informal, attempt to give the Soviet Union a sphere of influence in Eastern Europe would, as soon as the agreement became known, have brought a loud and effective outcry from our own Poles and Czechs.

I had more hope than Kennan that the Yalta Conference might produce some kind of workable agreement. All the subjects were going to be discussed by the three leaders. I do not think that I had any illusions that the end of the war would usher in an era of good feeling between the Allies and the Soviet Union. Like Kennan, I knew too much about the Soviet Union to believe that. At the same time, my contacts with Roosevelt and Hopkins had tempered my realism about Bolshevism with a political fact of life. As hopeless as the outlook seemed, the United States must try to get along with the Soviets. The American people, who had fought a long, hard war, deserved at least an attempt to work out a better world. If the attempt failed, the United States could not be blamed for not trying.

In short, foreign policy in a democracy must take into account the emotions, beliefs, and goals of the people. The most carefully thought-out plans of the experts, even though

100 percent correct in theory, will fail without broad public support. The good leader in foreign affairs formulates his policy on expert advice and creates a climate of public opinion to support it.[17]

Between February 1945 and February 22, 1946, when George Kennan's five-part "long cable" began to arrive in the State Department, the notion that the task of the West was to contain the outward thrust of Communist power rather than seek an agreed settlement embracing all of Europe had spread within the Foreign Service. Kennan's eloquent and influential essay helped crystallize that judgment in Washington. Its effect was perhaps heightened because its somewhat fevered prose was read on the pink cable forms which usually transmitted terse, professional messages. Kennan did not take the occasion to restate his earlier call for Eastern and Western spheres of influence, although two weeks later he reaffirmed it (see below, p. 44). In fact, his famous cable had remarkably little to say in specific terms about U.S. policy. But his portrait of implacable, hostile Soviet purposes and the need for "cohesion, firmness, and vigor" in the Western world, geared to "a constructive picture of the sort of world we would like to see," fitted well the views of those who envisaged a split of Europe and the formation of a Western bloc. Appendix D reproduces Kennan's "practical deductions" from his analysis of Soviet motives, intentions, and methods.

Although the process of exploration envisaged by Bohlen in his response to Kennan at Yalta proceeded in 1946, an increasing proportion of the relevant Foreign Service officers came to Kennan's conclusion about a split Europe. Advocates of Kennan's position tended to regard the offering of positive proposals to Moscow as a waste of time at best, dangerous at worst. There was, for example, an illuminating exchange between two senior Foreign Service officers in October 1946.[18]

On October 16 Robert Murphy, Clay's political adviser in

Berlin, cabled Washington expressing the view that the Soviets might be in such urgent need of German current production that, to get such reparations, they might be willing to open up their zone politically and be more receptive to steps toward German financial and economic unity. Murphy urged the U.S. to press this bargaining point: "This may be our last opportunity to use such a potent bargaining position in Germany for this purpose."

On October 23 Elbridge Durbrow, the chargé d'affaires in Moscow, responded by expressing doubt that such a move would secure any real Soviet political concessions regarding Germany: "It is characteristic of Kremlin practice to sacrifice an economic position rather than a political one whenever faced with necessity of making such a choice." He went on to argue that, even if the Soviets agreed to such concessions, the U.S. experience with regard to Eastern Europe indicated that the U.S.S.R. would withdraw those concessions, either overtly or covertly whenever long-term Soviet strategy dictated that step.

On October 25 Murphy responded by agreeing that extreme caution must be used in making any agreements with the U.S.S.R. but judging there was nothing to be lost in attempting negotiations along the line he had suggested. He warned against drawing too close a parallel between the German situation and the U.S. inability to influence developments or to secure Soviet compliance with existing agreements in Eastern Europe. Unlike the latter area, the U.S. had a prominent presence in Germany: "American policy has been to press for economic and political unification of Germany and not to be satisfied with unification of western zones. At some time test will come for all Germany and thus we are forced to gamble on whole rather than to fall back to defensive position in western zones alone. Accordingly, we believe that we must attempt to exploit any and all possibilities of opening up Soviet zones."

But Murphy, in the redoubtable atmosphere of Clay's Berlin, was rather the exception. The more typical view in the Foreign Service was that expressed by George Kennan in a cable from Moscow on March 6, 1946.[19] He argued bluntly that the Soviet effort was to achieve a Communist Germany, that the continued effort of the United States to achieve a united Germany was playing into Moscow's hands because its leaders were "quite confident that the Communists would be able to dominate a united Germany." Implicitly agreeing with this assessment, Kennan commended the buildup of the British and American zones "on relatively independent basis with constructive programs looking toward integration of these zones into general economic and political patterns of western Europe. . . ."

The anxiety in 1946 that pursuit of German unity would lead to a Soviet-dominated Germany was not confined to the American Foreign Service. It was a recurrent theme in French diplomatic exchanges with the United States, often linked to the notion of future American withdrawal of its effective weight from Europe.[20] For example, Murphy reported on February 24 that "members of the French delegation here [in Berlin] have admitted privately that present French policy is based not simply on fear of future German aggression but equally, if not more, on fear that the United States will lose interest, eventually withdraw from Germany, and that some fine morning they will wake up and find themselves face to face with the Russians on the Rhine."[21]

The British Foreign Office had, perhaps even earlier, come to the view that a permanently divided Germany was the best that could be wrested from the military and diplomatic situation that was emerging after the Second World War. Robert Murphy, in his memoir, reports that "the British decided very soon after Potsdam that Germany probably was permanently divided between East and West. . . ."[22]

By the spring of 1946, the Foreign Office view and the

dominant view of the senior officers in the U.S. embassy in Moscow were captured well in the following cable of May 31:[23]

761.00/5-3146: Telegram
The Ambassador in the Soviet Union (Smith)
to the Secretary of State
Secret   Moscow, May 31, 1946—10 a.m.
                                [Received May 31—7:16 a.m.]

1700. Views of British Foreign Office official expressed to Harriman (Dept's information circular airgram May 10).

We agree that Soviet satellite regimes are not likely to wither away. We do not minimize powerful domestic resentment against and opposition to these regimes, particularly in Poland, but we do wish to emphasize that in our opinion USSR is determined to continue domination over these states and is prepared to go to almost any lengths and employ almost any measures to achieve this end. Composition of satellite regimes may change but their essential subservience to USSR must, as far as Soviet intentions are concerned, continue.

We concur that USSR has not set any definite limits to its objectives in Europe and that only limitation on its activities are the opposition it encounters and the extent of its own capacities.

If foregoing is true then we are about to be driven into position—if we are not already there—where facts of situation compel us to view Europe not as a whole, but as divided essentially into two zones: a defensive one in the east where at best we can hope only to moderate Soviet dispensation, and a second zone in the west which has still not been brought under Soviet domination and in which there is still opportunity for USA and UK to nourish and support growth of healthy society reasonably immune and resistant to totalitarian virus.

Smith

Although its accent and emphasis were different, a similar schismatic view of the appropriate outcome in Europe was forming in what, for want of a better term, is called the liberal wing of the Democratic party. It was reflected, for example, in Henry Wallace's speech on foreign policy of September 12, 1946, which led to his being removed by Truman from his post as secretary of commerce at Byrnes' insistence. After providing a rationale out of Russian history for Moscow's concern with its security in Eastern Europe and eastern Germany and blaming the British as well as the Russians for conducting postwar power politics, Wallace called for a formal recognition of the split of Germany and Europe and an understanding between the United States and the Soviet Union about subsequent behavior:

> The real peace treaty we now need is between the United States and Russia. On our part, we should recognize that we have no more business in the *political* affairs of Eastern Europe than Russia has in the *political* affairs of Latin America, Western Europe and the United States. We may not like what Russia does in Eastern Europe. Her type of land reform, industrial expropriation, and suppression of basic liberties offends the great majority of the people of the United States. But whether we like it or not the Russians will try to socialize their sphere of influence just as we try to democratize our sphere of influence. This applies also to Germany and Japan. We are striving to democratize Japan and our area of control in Germany, while Russia strives to socialize eastern Germany. . . .
>
> The Russians have no more business in stirring up native communists to political activity in Western Europe, Latin America and the United States than we have in interfering in the politics of Eastern Europe and Russia. We know what Russia is up to in Eastern Europe, for example, and Russia knows what we are up to. We cannot permit the door to be closed against our trade in Eastern Europe any more than we can in China. But at the same time we have to recognize that the Balkans are closer to Russia than to us—and that Russia cannot permit either England or the United States to dominate the politics of that area. . . .

> Russia must be convinced that we are not planning for
> war against her and we must be certain that Russia is not
> carrying on territorial expansion or world domination
> through native communists faithfully following every twist
> and turn in the Moscow party line.[24]

In a curious way the Wallace position and that of the Foreign Service were identical, with one not trivial exception: Wallace assumed that a treaty assuring Soviet good behavior on the non-Communist side of the line was negotiable; the Foreign Service, regarding this concept as naïve, assumed (to use Kennan's phrase in his letter to Bohlen) that we would have to "keep the Russians out of" our sphere.

As the issue of policy toward the Soviet Union emerged in the first half of 1946, Truman took an independent initiative, as his earlier confidence that he and Stalin could work things out waned. In June he ordered his special counsel, Clark Clifford, to survey expert opinion in the government and report on the state of Soviet motivations, policies, and apparent intentions. Clifford's top secret report to the president, "American Relations with the Soviet Union," is dated September 24, 1946.[25] In seventy-nine pages, Clifford covered six subjects: Soviet foreign policy; Soviet-American agreements, 1942 to 1946; violations of Soviet agreements with the United States; conflicting views on reparations; Soviet activities affecting American security; and United States policy toward the Soviet Union. After evoking Soviet motivation and ambitions, along the lines of Kennan's February 1946 cable, the record of broken agreements, Soviet activities against U.S. interests beyond Eastern Europe, and the buildup of Soviet military strength, Clifford's recommendations included the following:

> The Soviet Government will never be easy to "get along
> with." The American people must accustom themselves to
> this thought, not as a cause for despair, but as a fact to be
> faced objectively and courageously. If we find it impossible

to enlist Soviet cooperation in the solution of world problems, we should be prepared to join with the British and other Western countries in an attempt to build up a world of our own which will pursue its own objectives and will recognize the Soviet orbit as a distinct entity with which conflict is not predestined but with which we cannot pursue common aims. . . .

Unless the United States is willing to sacrifice its future security for the sake of "accord" with the U.S.S.R. now, this government must, as a first step toward world stabilization, seek to prevent additional Soviet aggression. The greater the area controlled by the Soviet Union, the greater the military requirements of this country will be. Our present military plans are based on the assumption that, for the next few years at least, Western Europe, the Middle East, China and Japan will remain outside the Soviet sphere. If the Soviet Union acquires control of one or more of these areas, the military forces required to hold in check those of the U.S.S.R. and prevent still further acquisitions will be substantially enlarged. That will also be true if any of the naval and air bases in the Atlantic and Pacific, upon which our present plans rest, are given up. This government should be prepared, while scrupulously avoiding any act which would be an excuse for the Soviets to begin a war, to resist vigorously and successfully any efforts of the U.S.S.R. to expand into areas vital to American security. . . .

It must be made apparent to the Soviet Government that our strength will be sufficient to repel any attack and sufficient to defeat the U.S.S.R. decisively if a war should start. The prospect of defeat is the only sure means of deterring the Soviet Union. . . .

In addition to maintaining our own strength, the United States should support and assist all democratic countries which are in any way menaced or endangered by the U.S.S.R. Providing military support in case of attack is a last resort; a more effective barrier to communism is strong economic support. Trade agreements, loans and technical missions strengthen our ties with friendly nations and are effective demonstrations that capitalism is at least the equal of communism. The United States can do much to ensure that economic opportunities, personal freedom and social equality are made possible in countries outside the Soviet sphere by generous financial assistance. Our policy on reparations should be directed toward strengthening the areas we are endeavoring to keep outside the Soviet sphere. Our efforts to break down trade barriers, open up rivers and international waterways, and bring about economic unification of countries, now divided by occupation armies, are also directed toward the re-establishment of vigorous and healthy non-communist economies. . . .

Our policies must also be global in scope. By time-honored custom, we have regarded "European Policy," "Near Eastern Policy," "Indian Policy" and "Chinese Policy" as separate problems to be handled by experts in each field. But the areas involved, far removed from each other by our conventional standards, all border on the Soviet Union and our actions with respect to each must be considered in the light of overall Soviet objectives.

Only a well-informed public will support the stern policies which Soviet activities make imperative and which the United States Government must adopt. The American people should be fully informed about the difficulties in getting along with the Soviet Union, and the record of Soviet evasion, misrepresentation, aggression and militarism should be made public.

In conclusion, as long as the Soviet Government adheres to its present policy, the United States should maintain military forces powerful enough to restrain the Soviet Union and to confine Soviet influence to its present area. All nations not now within the Soviet sphere should be given generous economic assistance and political support in their opposition to Soviet penetration. Economic aid may also be given to the Soviet Government and private trade with the U.S.S.R. permitted provided the results are beneficial to our interests and do not simply strengthen the Soviet program. We should continue to work for cultural and intellectual understanding between the United States and the Soviet Union but that does not mean that, under the guise of an exchange program, communist subversion and infiltration in the United States will be tolerated. . . .

Even though the Soviet leaders profess to believe that the conflict between Capitalism and Communism is irreconcilable and must eventually be resolved by the triumph of the latter, it is our hope that they will change their minds and work out with us a fair and equitable settlement when they realize that we are too strong to be beaten and too determined to be frightened.

This paper, no doubt carefully read by Truman, foreshadows the Truman Doctrine, elements in the Marshall Plan, and a good deal more in future U.S. foreign policy. From the perspective of this chapter, it also reflects a fatalistic acceptance of the split of Europe.

This, then, was the emerging climate of opinion in which the Acheson-Clayton proposal to Byrnes was formulated.

4. How the Acheson-Clayton Plan Came to Be Formulated

One of the liveliest, most relaxed documents ever to be published among the solemn papers in *Foreign Relations of the United States* is a memorandum for the files on the origins of the Marshall Plan.[26] It was written by Charles Kindleberger, who had been much involved in the evolution of the plan. It is dated July 22, 1948, when the European Recovery Program, approved by Congress in April, was a going concern. Kindleberger evidently wrote from memory, without going back to the files. At one point he says: "In early 1946, Walt Rostow had a revelation that the unity of Germany could not be achieved without the unity of Europe, and that the unity of Europe could best be approached crabwise through technical cooperation in economic matters, rather than bluntly in diplomatic negotiations."

I would not quite rate my memorandum which went forward to Clayton on February 25, 1946, a revelation (for text, see Appendix A), and I would describe the strategy it incorporated in somewhat different terms, since it transcended "technical cooperation in economic matters." But it did represent the crystallization in my mind of a line of approach quite different from the one we had been taking in GA; its scope far exceeded our bureaucratic mandate; and it no doubt startled Kindleberger, whose deputy I then was, and my other colleagues. But we soon made common cause.

Several of us from the Office of Strategic Services (OSS),

who had worked on aspects of the German economy during the war, were drawn into the State Department on the grounds that our expertise was transferable to problems of occupation and reconstruction. Five former members of the Enemy Objectives Unit (EOU) of the U.S. embassy in London were among those recruited: Charles Kindleberger, John De Wilde, Harold Barnett, William Salant, and myself. We took the wry view that there was a certain rude justice in all this; having helped through our work on bombing target selection to knock the place down, it was fair enough to ask us to help rebuild it. About half the members of GA were drawn from outside EOU, including two hired fresh from the navy. At a higher bureaucratic level, Emile Despres and (later) Edward Mason of OSS also served under Clayton, the latter becoming his deputy and, later, Marshall's chief economic adviser at the Moscow conference of 1947. John Kenneth Galbraith, fresh from the Strategic Bombing Survey, served for a time in 1946 as office director, presiding over the divisions concerned with Japanese as well as German-Austrian economic policy. I came to work in the State Department the day the Potsdam communiqué was published. On receiving the document and then talking with colleagues returned from the Potsdam meetings, we quickly appreciated that the result was schizophrenic and, depending on what subsequently transpired, might lead to either German unity or split. By and large, we aligned ourselves with Clay and those backstopping his operation in Washington who sought to maximize the chance for German unity.

Our work, however, did not concern directly issues of high strategy. I, for example, concentrated on problems of German coal production and export. This involved reasonably important matters. From 1945 to 1946 and for several years thereafter the availability of coal, especially coking coal for steel, determined the rate of recovery of a number of the economies of Western Europe and Yugoslavia. I also played an ancillary role on the level-of-industry reparations issue and had in my domain one of the most complex and frustrating issues encountered in postwar years: the settlement of claims on German assets in Austria.

Our work moved forward, day by day, reaching interim crystallization in the policy document released by the State Department on December 12, 1945 (see above, p. 20). This reflected an accord among the three major working groups in Washington dealing with German occupation problems and their senior officers: EUR, GA, and the initially military (later State Department) unit (headed by General John Hilldring) which supported the occupation authorities in Germany, Austria, and Japan.

It was in the wake of that effort that a series of dissatisfactions converged in my mind to yield the initial memorandum in Appendix A and its subsequent elaborations. They took the form of an array of questions which current U.S. policy failed to answer. I am reasonably sure of what they were; but, as every historian knows, it is extremely uncertain business to reconstruct the past without valid documents; and the intellectual origins of a memorandum are, inherently, difficult to recapture, even one's own.

Two fundamental questions were raised by my participation in the Franco-American conversations held in Washington November 13 to 20, 1945.[27] The first was, simply, the appropriate long-run relationship of Germany to the rest of Europe. The French team, headed by Couve de Murville, came to make the case, as it did also in London and Moscow, for the detachment of the Ruhr-Rhineland area from the rest of Germany, to be placed under a special international authority independent of the Control Council in Berlin. At this time the French government was withholding its support from the Potsdam provisions for the setting up of central German administrative units until the Ruhr-Rhineland issue was settled. As the reigning Washington working-level expert on German coal production, I was invited along to some of the sessions despite my quite junior status in the State Department.

The French presented the case with their usual logic, precision, and elegance. But I found the piece of surgery they proposed unsatisfactory and unrealistic. By removing Germany's major industrial base, it would have not only radically reduced Germany's economic potential, already attenuated by the transfer of Silesia to Poland, but also would have provided a long-run focus for revived German resentment; and, besides, the proposal was unlikely to commend itself to Britain, the Soviet Union, or the United States. On the other hand, the underlying question had to be answered: how should the countries of Europe dependent on German coal exports, in particular, its industrial capacity in general, be assured for the long pull that Germany's inevitable economic bargaining power would not be translated into inappropriate bilateral political bargaining power? My thoughts turned to a long-run institutionalization of the already existing European Coal Organization (ECO), operating to allocate coal from European sources, including Poland, and from the United States. The further thought developed that, if institutions of economic unity on a wider front could emerge, embracing the European Central Inland Transport Organization (ECITO), in which the Soviet Union also participated, and the Emergency Economic Committee for Europe (EECE), a revived and united Germany might be safely fitted into Europe. It was already evident that those three ad hoc organizations, which had emerged in the wake of the armies advancing from the west, provided a forum in which the smaller countries, by combining their interests, could insist on evenhanded standards of equity in a way that simple bilateralism might not permit.

The second question, posed informally by the French, was that cited earlier (see above, p. 44): how was the security of France to be guaranteed vis-à-vis a united Germany, perhaps

Soviet-dominated, if an effective U.S. role in Europe was withdrawn? The question of America's staying in power in Europe was endemic in diplomatic conversations of late 1945 and early 1946, but it was sharply focused in the off-the-record exchanges on the French Ruhr-Rhineland proposals.[28]

The role of European unity was raised with me in December 1945 from a quite different direction. In discussing the State Department's policy document of December 9, which had just been published, my brother, Eugene, said, in effect: "This is all very well, but it won't work unless Germany is part of a united Europe."[29] The economic situation in Europe, quite aside from the dreadful condition of life in Germany, cried out for rapid German revival. But only a united Europe was likely to have the inner confidence and strength to receive and balance a revived Germany. Thus, my brother's criticism of our policy document converged with my reflections on the Franco-American conversations of the previous month.

The same theme emerged naturally from my work on the German assets issue in Austria. By a somewhat mysterious diplomatic process, the Russians had acquiesced in quite different arrangements for Austria than for Germany. In Germany, the members of the Allied Control Council could act unilaterally in their zones, within the limits of their various interpretations of the Potsdam agreements, but any policy applying to all of Germany had to be agreed unanimously in the Control Council. In effect, a veto applied. In Austria a national government was permitted to emerge through free elections with secret ballot by September 1945. The decisions of that government were to be final unless vetoed by unanimous agreement of the four occupying powers.[30] In 1945 and 1946 Austria was by no means a free, sovereign country. There were strong inhibitions on Austrian freedom of action and grave human difficulties, notably in the Soviet Zone of occupation. Moreover, the people, especially in the cities, were exceedingly poor and hungry. But they did have an increasingly effective democratic government of their own.

As I worked on the problems of Austria, against the background of the possible or even likely split of Germany and Europe, I asked myself this question: in the long run, how can this small country be viable if East and West split? Its optimum fate would be to live and trade with East and West, joined in an all-European collaboration. But, in any case, Austria had to become part of some larger economic unit if it was to be viable, and, evidently, a rejoining of Germany and Austria was not a possible political answer.

Another strand emerged from narrow economic analysis. As the position of the British and Continental economies became increasingly clear, it was palpable that a vastly larger flow of American aid to Europe would be required and for a much longer period than anyone had yet envisaged if Europe was, in fact, fully to recover. If this were to happen, however, a new basis for U.S. congressional support would be required. This lesson was driven home to all of us by the intense effort required to achieve the rather grudging passage by Congress of the special loan to Britain. The appeal in terms of British requirements and its wartime service to the Allied cause in standing alone from 1939 to 1941 only barely succeeded. It was clear that, if additional U.S. aid to Europe was going to be organized, it would have to be in terms of a large enterprise that looked forward rather than backward.

Finally, there was gathering evidence that Stalin viewed the postwar world as an arena of opportunity with the limits of that opportunity not yet set and, evidently, dependent in good part on his assessment of what the United States was prepared to do. That judgment was reinforced every day by the cables and intelligence reports chronicling the enterprising activities of the Soviet Union and its agents in Eastern Europe, Western Europe, and elsewhere; but it was given confirmation in Stalin's so-called electoral address of February 9, 1946. He held out to the peoples of the Soviet Union a rather grim vision of continued concentration on the buildup of heavy industry at home, framed by an explanation of the inherent tendency of the capitalist world to breed conflict and war. There was not a word encouraging the hope that continued collaboration among the wartime Allies might assure the peace. I concluded that it was essential to establish the extent to which this forbidding stance was based on the assumption of progressive U.S. withdrawal from Europe; and, if it were not, and if it represented fixed purposes irrespective of U.S. policy, a much more vigorous and purposeful U.S. policy was, in any case, required.

To all these strands was added a sense that, with no one quite willing it, the negotiations in Berlin and over the peripheral treaties were moving us step by step to a split Europe and a long-term East-West confrontation.

Just what brought these elements all together and induced me to set down the proposals, I simply do not recall. In sending the memorandum forward to Kindleberger, I simultaneously gave a copy to James Riddleberger of EUR. That occasion I remember well. I delivered and explained its background at his home in Chevy Chase on a Sunday. His Dutch wife was present and responded more positively than her husband to my vision of how a drive for a united Europe might help solve some of the problems for which none of us yet had satisfactory answers.

After a generally benign response within Clayton's domain, including Galbraith, the second version of the plan, geared to the forthcoming foreign minister's meeting, was formulated. It was at this stage that Jean Monnet was brought into the act. He was in Washington with Leon Blum, negotiating assistance for the French modernization plan. This occupied eleven weeks, starting on March 19, 1946.[31] He was thus in town in the period after our advocacy of European unity had been formulated and during the time when it moved up to Byrnes. I met Monnet not in connection with the French loan talks but because of his friendship with my brother, Eugene, stemming from their days together in North Africa in 1943. We talked in general terms about the theme of my memorandum, but my clearest memory of our conversation was his response to my remark that the American people deserved a better foreign policy than they were getting. Monnet said: "As a democrat with a small 'd' you cannot say that. In a democracy people can always gather in the town squares and insist on a good policy." Knowing in April that the latest and most operational form of our proposal was moving up to higher levels, I informed my brother and asked his advice. He came down to Washington and talked to Monnet in, as he recalls, the garden of the French embassy. Monnet supported the plan and so informed Acheson.

So much by way of anecdote.

The substantive question arises: why did James Dunn, H. Freeman Matthews, James Riddleberger, and other serious, knowledgeable officials oppose the plan? In part, I am sure, it was for the reasons I tried to evoke earlier (pp. 38–45)—that is, they felt Soviet intentions were expansionist, they had already written off Eastern Europe, including eastern Germany, and the best outcome they could envisage was a split Europe, with a Western bloc emerging. They had long since concluded that negotiations with the Soviet Union were fruitless and might open up the West to extensions of Soviet power. And, to a degree, they mistrusted the soundness and steadiness of Truman and Byrnes' vision of Soviet intentions. They feared that elements of naïveté persisted concerning the possibility of general negotiated settlements. In short, they tended to identify the split of Europe with a tough policy toward the Soviet Union, efforts to avoid the split as, in some sense, soft.

Put another way, I believe the senior members of the Foreign Service believed that their primary mission in 1946 was to educate American leaders in the nature of Soviet intentions. Frederick Nolting, who migrated from GA to the political side of the State Department, recalls, for example, that his colleagues were enormously pleased by Byrnes' speech in September in Stuttgart as evidence that the secretary of state had finally come to grips with the reality of Soviet intentions. He describes the mood as: "Thank God, Byrnes is at last wise to the Russian menace." [32] Bohlen's summation of Byrnes' task as secretary of state is in the same vein: "He had to shift from a wartime alliance to a policy of facing up to the emerging Soviet menace." [33] And, as Acheson succinctly put it: "The year 1946 was for the most part a year of learning that minds in the Kremlin worked very much as George F. Kennan had predicted they would." [34]

Those initiating the Acheson-Clayton proposal of April 1946 took a somewhat different view. We took it for granted that Stalin was intent on pressing Soviet power as far as he safely could; we were acutely aware that the position of the United States, in its widest sense, tended to encourage him to aim high; we were conscious that the assets and inherent strength of the United States had not been effectively mobilized to indicate the options that the Soviet Union would eventually face; and our proposal was meant to try to mobilize those assets. We were, moreover, sensitive to the likely costs of a split Europe: the loss of human freedoms for those in Eastern Europe, where the struggle, as of February to April 1946, had by no means been wholly lost; a perpetual confrontation and arms race on either side of the line; a United Nations bedeviled and weakened by that confrontation for which, once consolidated, we could see no end. We thought all this would be a pretty poor outcome for those in the Soviet Union as well as the West who had fought and died in the recent struggle. We understood the EUR argument that all-German institutions and an all-European settlement would offer the Soviet Union room for maneuver in the West as well as Western influence in the East, but we rejected the notion that the United States—and the West as a whole—was incapable of coping with such Soviet efforts. As far as Germany was concerned, this was the view of Clay and the Americans on the Control Council staff. In short, we believed that acceptance of the split was a weak, not a strong, policy. We did not know whether our proposals could succeed, but we believed that, in the American interest and the general human interest, they were worth a college try.

All this lies behind the following memorandum from Kindleberger to Benjamin Cohen, perhaps Byrnes' closest adviser on the treaties, who, while of considerable independence of mind, took a view which converged with that of EUR as far as peace treaty strategy was concerned.

c—Mr. Cohen   April 5, 1946
GA—Mr. C. P. Kindleberger

I have reflected on our discussion of Monday concerning the role of the element of power in our European diplomacy. I take it to be your position that our present program of piecemeal negotiation is likely to produce, over a period of time, a European settlement more satisfactory than any that might result from an immediate effort to set forth and agree broad terms for a united Europe, combined with proposed settlement, within those terms, of the major outstanding issues.

In the light of your judgment I have reviewed the major issues that fall within the knowledge of GA. They include, I believe, a substantial proportion of our outstanding major European problems, and appear to reflect faithfully the nature of the forces now at work in Europe.

In the light of that review I would submit to you again the following observations:

1. Both USSR and UK, as well as France, are now proceeding on the assumption that Europe will, in fact, split, and they assume this in large part because they feel the US interest in the European structure is transitory.

2. This assumption tends to maximize the power element in every European issue, no matter how inconsequential.

3. In terms of this assumption the US struggle to achieve some degree of independence for Austria, by opposing USSR

infiltration, its program of protest and obstruction, where possible in Eastern Europe, can only appear to USSR as part of a long-run effort to corrupt the East European bloc. It is significant that a Russian is recently reported to have remarked that our protest against USSR economic policy in Eastern Europe is judged in Moscow as an effort to preserve markets and economic influence for Germany. Although US policy in fact may be motivated by a conception of independence within the UNO, as a substitute for the older tradition of East Europe as a satellite area to a major power, nothing in the present organization of the UNO offers the guarantee that exclusive blocs will not form in Europe, and very little of US diplomatic action in Europe could be interpreted as offering a realistic alternative to blocs. It is significant that USSR interpreted our delay in decision over the Rhineland-Ruhr as a tacit connivance in a Western bloc conception; and that the UK regards the compromises we forced on them, to achieve agreement on the level of industry as a romantic concession to the Eastern bloc.

4. In fact, to the extent that US policy can be distinguished from UK policy in Europe, that distinction arises from the One Europe assumption that characterized Yalta and parts of the Potsdam Agreement. It seems clear to us, in the light of the character of day-to-day diplomacy that we must either re-assert our faith in a European solution, other than relatively exclusive blocs; or we must, increasingly, find ourselves, *de facto*, in support of the British bloc conception.

5. We recognize, of course, that the type of diplomatic offensive we advocate would be subjected to the most intense and suspicious scrutiny, not only by the UK, but also by France, and the USSR. Its terms would have to be drafted in such a way that, initially, they would involve no relative surrender, by East or West; but rather equal surrender to the larger forum. Over a period of time, it would be the hope that the power or security element, within such a forum, would diminish, by a succession of equal withdrawals. To the West the guarantee of US participation, and to the East the assertion of US interest might well make this solution

acceptable. We appreciate that the tactics of diplomacy required, including prior consultation at a high level with USSR and UK, would be fairly delicate.

6. In short, we doubt that the present array of negotiations in Europe—against a background of assumed split, with no operating tie-up to the UNO machinery, and with the long-run US interest heavily discounted—is likely to prove fruitful of results consistent with large US interests.

Behind the difference in perspective between EUR and GA lay differences in training and experience. The stance of EUR was wholly consonant with the tradition of diplomacy in general, American diplomacy in particular. A diplomat reports the situations he sees about him in foreign areas and the professional conversations in which he engages. He negotiates on the basis of instructions dispatched to him from the capital. When assigned to headquarters, he advises those bearing political responsibility on the appropriate policies to adopt, in the light of his nation's interests and the exact current situation in particular foreign areas, and dispatches the resulting instructions to the field. The traditional diplomat is engaged in a bookish sort of job: a job of reading, writing, thinking, and talking to others like himself. He does not command masses of men, manipulate complicated machines, or deploy large economic resources. He is trained to report accurately and with perception and, above all, to communicate with as near absolute lucidity as possible.

The American diplomatic tradition began, of course, with important business: the protection of the young nation's interests during the War of Independence, the years of weakness under the Articles of Confederation, and the dangerous complexities of the period of the French Revolution and the Napoleonic Wars, as well as the War of 1812. And these contentious years drew a good many distinguished men into American diplomacy: Franklin, Livingston, Jay, Jefferson, Randolph, Pickering, and the two Adamses. But then came a long, relatively quiet time.

The ease with which American interests could be protected after 1815 in the world arena of the nineteenth century, behind the shield of the British navy, was reflected in the scale of American diplomatic operations. Two clerks worked for Livingston when he tried to manage foreign affairs under the Articles of Confederation; a chief clerk with seven subordinates served John Quincy Adams; and the staff of the Department of State numbered less than a hundred as late as the beginning of the twentieth century.

Over the previous decades, the number of missions abroad increased, as did the number of incoming and outgoing messages. The typewriter superseded the painfully transcribed and copied dispatch; wireless, for many purposes, superseded the sea pouch; but there was a true continuity in the Department of State's business. For the most part, it handled a steady flow of two-way communications concerning the commercial and other private problems in which American citizens traveling or conducting business abroad became involved; and it noted and filed the endless flow of dispatches forwarded by those on foreign service, describing the state of things in the parts of the world to which they were assigned.

In 1794 John Quincy Adams defined the role of the American diplomat as follows: "It is our duty to remain the peaceful and silent though sorrowful spectators of the European scene."[35] Sorrowful or not, the American representative abroad had to become the detached analyst of a set of relationships which it was the interest of his nation intermittently to exploit while avoiding sustained involvement. This posture persisted, as we shall see, well into the twentieth century.

Down to the First World War (and even to 1939), the great acts of foreign policy—the issues which get into the books on diplomatic history—were so few and far between that they were handled personally by the secretary of state, usually in intimate consultation with the president, or they were directly handled by the president himself. At the most, each administration of the nineteenth century is associated with only two or three such major diplomatic affairs, usually in the form of a negotiated treaty, but twice (the Monroe Doctrine and the Open Door) a unilaterally enunciated statement of American policy.

Reflecting changes in the nation's outlook and style which had been gathering force in the latter decades of the nineteenth century, American diplomacy began to move toward a new maturity after 1900. Elihu Root was the father of the modern Department of State as well as of the modern American army. His reforms in 1905 and 1906 usefully mark the moment when the modern American professional diplomatic tradition was founded. Its subsequent development lagged behind the rise in de facto American power on the world scene. Nevertheless, the Department of State, along with its Foreign Service, was a quite different institution on the eve of Pearl Harbor than it had been when John Hay dispatched the Open Door notes.

The Foreign Service came to be based on a civil service merit system, and a few of the universities began systematically to train young men for diplomacy. The process of maturing was carried forward by the experience of the First World War. The tangled issues arising in its early stages from American neutrality were, on the whole, well handled, the Department of State being the president's diplomatic instrument for these narrow purposes. When, however, the United States became a belligerent and then assumed major responsibility for the making of peace, Wilson looked elsewhere for his staff work. A special group under Edward House was created in 1917 to prepare for the peace conference; and the secretary of state, Robert Lansing, acquiesced in this arrangement, which basically divorced the Department of State from the peace-making process.

The First World War and its immediate aftermath did not, then, significantly develop the Department of State as an instrument of staff work or planning in foreign policy. It did, however, expand the cumulative professional experience of the department in the technical business of modern diplomacy, and the nation's withdrawal of commitment after 1920 brought the level of the nation's problems and responsibilities in foreign affairs back to the low, but rising, level of the State Department's competence. Perhaps the most important positive effect of the First World War and its aftermath on the development of American diplomacy was to draw into the department a new generation of able men whose imagination was caught by the Foreign Service and who concluded from the events of 1914 to 1920 that the American role in foreign affairs would eventually expand. And in the postwar decade Charles Evans Hughes and Henry Stimson carried forward in the Root tradition. From 1920 to 1933, within the narrow limits of American foreign policy, the professional service developed steadily in stature. Among those who entered the field of diplomacy during the First World War and in the decade thereafter and later achieved distinction were Norman Armour (1915), Sumner Wells (1915), Allen Dulles (1916), Stanley Hornbeck (1918), William Castle (1919), James Dunn (1920), John Hickerson (1920), Herschel Johnson (1920), Robert Murphy (1920), H. Freeman Matthews (1924), George Kennan (1926), Charles Bohlen (1929), and James Riddleberger (1929).

With the Roosevelt administration forces came into play which radically altered the role of the Department of State and the American diplomatic tradition. Unlike his three immediate predecessors, Roosevelt was actively interested in the details of diplomacy as well as in broad foreign policy positions. He was unwilling to delegate day-to-day operations to the same degree as Harding, Coolidge, and Hoover; and, like Wilson, he was not prepared to regard the secretary of state as his sole agent in foreign affairs. Franklin Roosevelt regarded Cordell Hull as a responsible adviser over only a limited area of foreign policy and the Foreign Service as an instrument of limited usefulness to him. It was Hull's position in relation to the Senate that mainly commended him to the president. This was an important link which became increasingly important as the diplomacy of the Second World War came to its climax; but the truly revolutionary factor which progressively affected the role of the Department of State was that the United States began to throw into the world power balance its military, economic, political, and psychological weight.

In early 1941 the United States began military and economic negotiations with the British. By the time of Pearl Harbor or shortly thereafter the Department of State was surrounded by a Treasury pressing hard distinctive lines of foreign policy, the Lend-Lease Administration, the Board of Economic Warfare, the Office of Strategic Services, and a White House group headed by Harry Hopkins. In addition, those charged with war production and shipping responsibilities had their hands on important levers of foreign policy which they often used with vigor on their own initiative. Moreover, within the Department of State the Foreign Service (numbering about eight hundred) was all but engulfed by men on temporary appointment who were doing special jobs arising from the war effort.

The coordination of this sprawling foreign affairs empire lay uniquely in the president's hands. Although the Department of State itself expanded greatly in the course of the war years, and its personnel shared many of the adventures and enterprises of the time, its monopoly position under the president was broken, never to be fully regained in the postwar decades.

As their memoirs reveal, Robert Murphy, Charles Bohlen, and George Kennan—and many of their Foreign Service colleagues—were much more than passive observers of the scene during and immediately after the Second World War; but, still, they operated in a context where the political, military, and economic levers of American power were in the hands of others. George Kennan once captured this sense of

inherent limitation in American diplomacy extraordinarily
well:

> Essentially what the diplomat does is only to maintain
> communication with other governments about the behavior
> of the respective countries in ways that have reciprocal
> impacts and are of interest to the governments. The diplo-
> mat writes notes and holds discussions, under the President's
> authority, with other governments, *about* America's behav-
> ior as a nation among nations. But he himself has no direct
> control over this behavior—he merely talks about it, defines
> it, explains it, listens to protests about it, and expresses
> whatever undertakings he is permitted to express about its
> future nature. He is only the clerk and the recorder—a
> secretary, of sorts—not an independent agent. For every real
> promise or commitment he expresses to a foreign govern-
> ment regarding the behavior of the U.S. on the international
> scene, he must have the sanction of some domestic authority
> which has the corresponding real power and is prepared to
> back him up.
>
> When, therefore, the military used to say to us: this or that
> must be obtained by "diplomatic means," they were using
> an empty term. Strictly speaking, there are no diplomatic
> means, divorced from the real elements of national power
> and influence, which are all—in the U.S.—remote from dip-
> lomatic control.[36]

This deeply rooted image of the diplomat's task and its limitations substantially explains, I believe, why the senior European experts of the Foreign Service undertook as their
central mission in 1946 to educate the president, the secretary of state, and the foreign policy establishment, generally,
in the realities of Soviet thought and policy. As they observed
the ambiguities and uncertainties of American policy, they
regarded that mission as serious and fundamental; but it was
not for them to define the military, political, and economic
consequences and requirements for bringing that mission to
completion.

The young men in GA did not instinctively accept the limitations Kennan described. It was this sense that the framework within which we operated was subject to change and manipulation, including the domestic political base, that distinguished us from our Foreign Service colleagues. We were comfortable with operations that transcended the narrow terrain of diplomacy. Our experience in public policy had been relatively brief and narrow; but it had involved making an appreciation of the situation, defining goals, and helping design courses of action to achieve them. As economists, we understood one of the major instruments that had to be brought to bear, and we knew something as well about military power. I remember well my reaction to reading Kennan's long cable of February 22 as it came across my desk in delayed installments: "OK, but what are we going to do about it?" And, by the time I read that cable, I had already defined and recently sent forward my notion of what ought to be done.

But our effort of February to April 1946 clearly failed. The year 1946 was taken up not with the launching of our proposed enterprise to attempt to forestall the split of Europe but with a series of tests of Soviet intentions. In Eastern Europe, did the Soviet Union intend to live up to the Yalta commitments? In Berlin, did the Soviet Union intend to permit the creation of central economic agencies and a democratic Germany embracing the Soviet Zone? In the peripheral treaties, was the Soviet Union prepared for a sharing of power, East and West? In Germany, was the Soviet Union interested in a long-term disarmament treaty for a unified Germany? For EUR the negative responses to these questions were a satisfactory outcome of the educational process it took as its central task. For GA these negative responses foreshadowed an unsatisfactory, second-order outcome. We believed Soviet intentions depended to a significant degree on the Soviet view of what the United States intended to do; and we thought a satisfactory test of Soviet policy required a stance quite different from the defensive, uncertain, questioning American posture of 1946. That is what I had meant when I observed to Monnet—and was properly reprimanded—that the United States deserved a better foreign policy than it was getting. That is also what I had in mind in the concluding passages of my inaugural lecture at Oxford on November 12, 1946.[37] After evoking the potentially creative role of the United States in helping build federal structures in Europe and elsewhere, transcending old-fashioned nationalism, I went on:

> Then there are the other familiar strengths of the American position: the physical resources of the country; the depth and unbroken continuity of its democratic tradition; a history of successful, if occasionally slow and raucous, adjustment to new circumstances; a willingness to experiment; a constructive energy; a persistent strand of idealism. These are the assets which it is the task of American statesmanship effectively to mobilize. The structure of American political life does not make that task easy. Although the recent revolution of American diplomacy is likely to hold the United States actively in world affairs, fluctuations in the degree and efficacy of American intervention are to be expected.
>
> American history has been marked by only occasional periods when the full strength of the nation has been unified and made effective—usually in the face of crisis and under great leadership—but the intervening periods have not been without purpose.

It was not in 1946 but in the late winter and spring of 1947 that the full strength of the United States was unified and made effective, in the face of crisis and under great leadership, but by that time the forces making for the split of Europe were much stronger than they were a year earlier. And the building of a Western bloc proved the maximum attainable goal.

5. The ECE, the Crisis of 1947, and the Marshall Plan

But something did emerge from the Acheson-Clayton proposal: the United Nations Economic Commission for Europe (ECE) in Geneva, which triggered, in turn, the creation of regional economic commissions in Asia and the Far East, Latin America, and Africa. In addition, the proposal constitutes one strand in the complex skein of thought which yielded the Marshall Plan in 1947.

The ECE came to life in the following way. While high-level diplomacy was seized of the problems of Eastern Europe, the treaties, and Germany, the Economic and Social Council of the United Nations (ECOSOC) faced a more mundane issue.[38] The United Nations Relief and Rehabilitation Administration (UNRRA), agreed in 1943, had run its political course by early 1946. UNRRA had always been envisaged as an immediate postwar expedient, not a long-run institution. But, in any case, the American Congress was not in a mood to continue open-ended aid to Western Europe, let alone Eastern Europe and the Soviet Union. On the other hand, reconstruction in Europe was evidently not complete. A little time had been bought for Britain by the American loan granted by Congress in 1946, and Leon Blum and Jean Monnet had succeeded by the end of May 1946 in putting together a package of loans totaling about $1.5 billion in support of the French five-year modernization plan Monnet and his team had designed. In Eastern Europe, however, there was anxiety, notably in Warsaw and Prague, on two counts: the loss of aid from UNRRA and the fear, political as well as economic, that the evolving political shape of the region would break virtually all links to the West. Meanwhile, as noted earlier (p. 54), three functional instruments of European cooperation were doing business: ECO, ECITO, and the EECE.

It was against this background that ECOSOC announced on July 26, 1946, the creation of the Temporary Sub-Commission on the Economic Reconstruction of Devastated Areas. Its purpose was to survey Europe's need and to recommend appropriate courses of action. The twenty members of the commission were, formally, acting in their individual capacity, but they were in fact government representatives. The American member was Isador Lubin, supported by three advisers drawn from the federal bureaucracy: Harold van Buren Cleveland, Frederick Strauss, and John Gunter. They began their work in London on July 29, 1946.

Before the American team departed, I talked with Cleveland, suggesting that an Economic Commission for Europe might be a useful outcome of the subcommission's work, and I gave him a copy of the portion of the Acheson-Clayton plan that outlined such an institution. Cleveland responded positively, in part because, quite independently, he had been drawn toward the notion of European economic unity. In London, Lubin's team ran into some kindred American souls: the group in the U.S. embassy, headed by Paul R. Porter, which backstopped ECO, EECE, and ECITO (which actually met in Paris). Like Cleveland and me, Porter had come independently to the conclusion that institutions to consolidate economic cooperation in Europe were essential for political stability as well as economic revival. In Porter's case, the chain of logic ran from the need to revive fully the German economy to the institutional setting in which that revival would be consistent with political stability.[39] He was impressed by the vitality of European cooperation in the "E" organizations. It was, therefore, natural that Porter should be looking about for a long-term home for his technocratic clubs. Cleveland and Theodore Geiger, on Porter's staff, took an active role in lobbying for an Economic Commission for Europe.

They found an eager answering response in the Polish and Czech delegations. The ECE was, in fact, jointly proposed by the U.S., U.K., and Polish members, the British having abandoned earlier reservations.[40] By the time the work of the subcommission was finished, on September 13, 1946, the idea of an ECE had clear majority support. The Soviet Union and some other countries reserved their positions but did not obstruct the recommendation from going to the ECOSOC, where it was promptly considered. The Soviet reservation centered on the possibility that the ECE might interfere with the Control Council's powers in Germany. Due to Soviet opposition, the creation of the ECE was deferred, but, at the U.N. General Assembly meeting in December, ECOSOC was unanimously urged "to give prompt and favourable consideration to the establishment of an Economic Commission for Europe." Evidently, Soviet reservations had been reduced, but they were not eliminated. In March 1947, when the terms of reference of the ECE were drawn up by ECOSOC, the Soviet delegation sought to minimize contacts between the Control Council in Berlin and the new organization. When its view did not prevail, the Soviet delegation abstained on the final vote setting the ECE into motion on March 28, 1947. The Economic Commission for Asia and the Far East (ECAFE) was created by an ECOSOC resolution on the same day. Gunnar Myrdal has often observed that the ECE was created at "the very last moment" possible, given the rapid emergence of the Cold War in the first half of 1947.[41] I would agree.

Soviet participation in the ECE was in doubt until a large delegation turned up for the first session, in May 1947, in Geneva. Gunnar Myrdal was appointed executive secretary; ECO, ECITO, and EECE were absorbed and maintained their momentum at the committee level; but the initial meeting of the commission itself, which Will Clayton attended, was marked by a good deal of noisy polemics from the Soviet side. Clayton took away from the session an only partially accurate sense that the ECE was not likely to be a very congenial club.[42]

Meanwhile, on quite separate tracks, three forces were converging to bring the issue of European recovery and the larger question of European unity or schism to the center of the stage.

First was the abnormally severe winter of 1946–47, with the setback it caused in the economies of Western Europe (see above, pp. 29–37). This was brought home with particular force to Clayton, who spent considerable time in Geneva on trade negotiations and in London. In London he was in close touch with Paul Porter and his staff at the American embassy, who not only helped nurture the ECE into life but also followed, day by day, the vicissitudes of the European economy. Porter was Clayton's deputy at the first meeting of the ECE in Geneva.[43] He subsequently became the permanent representative of the United States to the organization. Clayton's most influential memorandum, which no doubt helped focus Washington's collective mind sharply, was based on notes made on a flight from Geneva to Washington May 19, 1947, completed and given to Marshall in Washington on May 27.[44]

Second was the Truman Doctrine, laid before Congress on March 12, 1947. The British inability to continue to carry the burden of supporting the Greek government in the face of externally supported guerrilla war dramatized its marginal financial position. Meanwhile, Turkey was under extremely heavy diplomatic pressure to cede the Soviet Union a role in the Dardanelles. The American initiative in response to this dual crisis encountered widespread criticism on the grounds that it was a negative and incomplete response to the dangers Europe faced, many of which were not of Moscow's contriving.

Third was the reaction of George Marshall, now secretary of state, to his protracted negotiations in Moscow on Germany in March and April 1947. He concluded—as had many others over the previous year and a half—that Stalin did not intend to move toward a unified democratic Germany, but he did not stop there. Unlike Byrnes he also concluded that the economic, social, and political disarray of Western Europe, with all the opportunities it appeared to open for Soviet penetration, was a major reason for Stalin's complacency in the face of delay over the German problem. As Joseph Jones reports, one lesson of Moscow was that "to deal with the problem of Germany it was necessary to deal with the problem of Europe."[45] Marshall clearly understood that the policy of the United States, as perceived by Moscow, was one determinant of Soviet policy. And he decided the United States would have to act. George Kennan paraphrases Marshall's pithy view as of April 29, 1947: "Europe was in a mess. Something would have to be done. If he [Marshall] did not take the initiative, others would."[46]

The origins and formative diplomacy of the Marshall Plan are by now well-trod historical ground.[47] As far as this book is concerned, only two points are to be noted. Those who had reacted positively to the proposal of February 25, 1946—and its various elaborations—were among those who helped shape the Marshall Plan proposal: Acheson and Clayton, above all; Kindleberger, Cleveland, and other economists in the State Department;[48] and, in the background, with special influence on Will Clayton over the winter of 1946–47, Paul Porter and his London staff. There was also, of course, George Kennan and his Policy Planning Staff, whose papers helped contribute two important elements to the Marshall Plan offer: the requirement that the Europeans bestir themselves to produce a coherent response and the opening left for the Soviet Union and the countries of Eastern Europe to join if they were so minded.[49]

As far as the Acheson-Clayton plan of April 1946 was concerned, all that can be said is that, to some limited degree impossible to measure, the formulation and circulation a year earlier of a recovery plan linking a European organization to enlarged American aid, plus the midwifery of bringing the ECE to life, may have contributed an element to the creative ferment that yielded the Marshall Plan as the something that had to be done, in the wake of the secretary of state's instruction; and that creative ferment, in part, was incorporated in a vital group of young economists who had, for a year and more, been contemplating the problem of European recovery and economic organization and were well prepared to contribute directly to the formulation of the Marshall Plan.

The second and major point bearing on the central problem addressed in this book, however, is that the prior existence of the ECE converged with Truman and Marshall's decision to give the possibility of an all-European settlement one more test. The documentary record shows clearly that, at the highest levels of government, the policy of the United States was to make that test in good faith.[50] The risks of Soviet and Eastern European participation in complicating the task both diplomatically and with Congress were, of course, recognized, but they were judged to be outweighed by the advantages of an all-European outcome. And, as in the case of German policy, it was judged to be important that the United States not be, in image or reality, the initiator of a split Europe. Molotov's performance in Paris, against the will of the Polish and Czechoslovak governments, assured that this would be the case.

6. A Few Reflections

Three questions are posed by the interplay of ideas and the sequence of events dealt with in this volume. First, how important was the formulation of the Acheson-Clayton plan to the emergence of the idea of European economic unity on both sides of the Atlantic in subsequent months and years? Second, if the plan had been accepted, is it likely that it could have been successfully launched in 1946 by the American political process? Third, if the plan had become American policy in 1946, is it likely that it would have been accepted by Stalin and averted the split of Europe?

In his *Economic Co-operation in Europe*, David Wightman remarks in reference to the Acheson-Clayton plan: "The foreign offices of Europe no doubt contain many memoranda similar to the one already described which was drafted in the State Department." Whether this is literally true or not, I believe Wightman is essentially correct. The concept of European unity goes back many centuries, and, as Winston Churchill noted in his Zurich speech (see Appendix F), Count Coudenhove-Calergi and Aristide Briand argued the case during the interwar years. The process resulting in the Acheson-Clayton plan was, as nearly as I know, the first formalization in the American government of the case for U.S. political and economic support for European economic unity, accompanied by distinctively European security arrangements; but, as Wightman implies, it would have been remarkable if the concept of European unity did not emerge in this period on both sides of the Atlantic. I once allowed myself the spacious generalization: "On occasion it may be proper to regard the course of history as inevitable, *ex post*; but not *ex ante*."[51] As nearly as the word "inevitable" has meaning in dealing with the chancy behavior of human beings and the institutions they create, the idea of European unity was destined to be a feature of the post-1945 world.

This is the case, I believe, because the ancient dream offered a partial solution, at least, to five major problems which converged in the wake of the Second World War; and the acceptance of major new courses of action often results from such convergence.

First, there was the general situation of Europe. The outcome of the Second World War shattered Europe's image of itself. For at least five centuries—since, say, the emergence of reasonably strong national states—Europe had been a kind of contentious Middle Kingdom of the West. It was often at war within itself; but its culture, ideas, and economic and military power gradually spread out over the face of the rest of the globe. It generated the scientific revolution and the industrial revolution. And despite the terrible costs of the First World War, despite the interwar vicissitudes, in 1939 Europeans still regarded themselves as standing at the center of the world. Five years later the Soviet Union was emplaced on the Elbe; the region from the Elbe to the Channel was totally dependent on the military and economic power of the United States; and Britain, despite its extraordinarily vital performance during the Second World War, was only in degree less dependent. It was clear to many in Europe that only in unity could their continent find the strength to deal in dignity and balance with the continental powers to the east and across the Atlantic.

Second, more particularly, many recognized that Europe could no longer afford inner contention. European nationalism had been granted a last fling during the interwar years, and it had failed. In Eastern Europe the Austro-Hungarian Empire had been broken up after the First World War. Poland, as well as the Baltic states, had been granted independence, but the arrangement had not proved viable in the cockpit of European power politics. Above all, thoughtful French and Germans, some reflecting on the fate of their nations in concentration camps and in underground movements, concluded that reconciliation was the only viable route to the survival of their national traditions and values and of the European heritage in a larger sense.

Third, there was the problem of Germany in relation to the rest of Europe. Despite total defeat and total postwar prostration, few doubted that, in one way or another, the visceral energy of the German people would reassert itself, and the German economy would rise again. A fully revived Germany, the largest country of Europe, well endowed with resources, astride the Continent's balance of power, was seen as a potential threat, even if disarmed, if it dealt with all the others on a bilateral basis. Evidently, one way to cope with that threat was to place relations with Germany, economic and, to a degree, political, in a framework of Continental unity.

Fourth, there were the economic problems. It obviously made sense for the European countries to cooperate in the struggle to reconstruct their economies. And, looking to the longer future, there was the lesson of what European economic nationalism had cost between the wars. There was also the lesson of the United States and the advantages it enjoyed because of its open, unified continental market, as well as the prospect of a second great continental economy emerging to full stature in the Soviet Union.

Finally, there was the problem of the relation of the United States to Europe. Some American leaders shared an understanding from a European perspective of the first four of these problems and the extent to which unity might contribute to solutions. But there was a distinctly American problem as well. Would the American people, whatever its ultimate interests might be, support a peace based once again on contentious European nationalism? The reemergence of assertive European nationalism after the First World War had helped create the mood in which Wilson lost the battle for American entrance into the League of Nations; although, surely, Wilson himself contributed to that result. But here, once again, were the Americans, reluctantly dragged by events out of an isolationism, whose unwisdom they were prepared to acknowledge, to help salvage Europe at great cost. Surely this time Americans would have to act more wisely; but surely, if they were to underwrite European recovery and security, they also had the right to ask Europeans to act more wisely. It was natural for Americans to echo, with respect to Europe, Thomas Paine's cry to his countrymen 170 years earlier: "Now is the seed-time of Continental Union."

Some of these strands ran through Churchill's reference to German and European unity in his Zurich speech on European unity of September 19, 1946, and John Foster Dulles' of January 17, 1947 (see Appendixes F and G). Both, formally at least, were careful to elaborate their arguments in terms of Europe as a whole, but the basic case could be made for Western Europe alone. Indeed, Churchill said: "If at first all states of Europe are not willing or able to join the union, we must nevertheless proceed to assemble and combine those who will and can." Much in the spirit of the Acheson-Clayton proposal, Dulles counseled that the major Allied powers should "think more in terms of the economic unity of Europe and less in terms of the Potsdam dictum that Germany shall be 'a single economic unit.' Of course, there should be an economic unification of Germany. But the reason for that is also a reason for the economic unification of Europe." All five of the problems cited above existed for Western Europe alone, which, after all, constituted two-thirds of the continent. In addition, of course, the possibility that the region might have to resist collectively encroachments from the east heightened the case.

Conceptually, then, the Acheson-Clayton plan of April 1946 may, in narrow bureaucratic terms, have been mildly precocious, but it belongs with a stream of thought gathering momentum in many minds.

If all-European or Western unity was an inevitable and proper component in the solution of Europe's postwar problems and also a potentially stable basis for the relations between the United States and Europe, the large questions posed by this book are these. Why did the United States government not accept and act on the Acheson-Clayton plan in the spring and summer of 1946? And, if the United States had so acted, could an all-European settlement have been achieved and the split of Europe avoided?

In terms of the limited arena of technical diplomacy, the answer to the first question is tolerably clear. The secretary of state did not adopt the approach Acheson and Clayton suggested. Operating within the limits of the situation as he found it, he "tested Soviet intentions": in the peripheral treaties, by supporting Clay in Berlin, by offering the long-term disarmament of a unified Germany. But he did not put credibly to the Soviet leadership a clear choice between an all-European or a Western bloc settlement backed by the full weight of American economic and, if necessary, military power. Nor did he seek seriously to support the cause of Polish democracy. And, as his term as secretary of state came to a close, the economy of Western Europe was retrogressing, Germany still a morass.

Byrnes did come to an assessment of "Soviet intentions," but he does not appear to have appreciated the extent to which those intentions were a function of the Soviet image of American intentions and capabilities. Without Clay's intervention he may well have removed from the Stuttgart speech the critical sentence affirming the U.S. intention to keep an occupation force in Germany as long as necessary. And behind that uncertainty, in turn, may have been the doubt that the United States would, in fact, do so.

Like the dog that didn't bark, one central fact in this story is that, as nearly as the files of the National Archives and the Truman Library reveal, as well as the memory of Truman's special counsel, Clark Clifford, the Acheson-Clayton proposal was never put to the president. It is evident that, if the image of U.S. intentions in Europe was to be altered and a sharp, credible choice laid before the Soviet leadership, the president would have to be centrally involved, just as he was to be in the formulation and execution a year later of the Truman Doctrine and the Marshall Plan. Only the president could have explained to the American people the slide toward a split Europe, the costs to the world and to the United States if it were consummated, the role in the process of the image of progressive U.S. withdrawal, the case for U.S. financial support for an all-European settlement, the need to proceed promptly with the West if the Soviet Union did not agree. Only he could have reasserted a continuity in U.S. policy toward Poland reaching back to Yalta, Hopkins' agreement with Stalin in May 1945, and the Potsdam agreement on Poland. A major turnaround in American policy would have been required. And only a president could have brought it about.

It is clear as a matter of fact that Byrnes did not accept the Acheson-Clayton proposal, and he pursued a quite different strategy in 1946, conforming to the views of EUR and his counselor, Benjamin Cohen. To a degree impossible to weigh, an element of personality may have entered his decision in this matter, for Byrnes' style and, perhaps, his prior relationship to Truman made him most reluctant to turn to the president. This is how Bohlen describes Byrnes' method of operation:

> Byrnes's personal style was to operate as a loner, keeping matters restricted to a small circle of advisers (of which I think I could call myself one). Thus he failed to get the most

out of the talent and expertise of the State Department. Moreover, he was not in daily, intimate consultation with the President, as Hopkins had been with Roosevelt and subsequent national-security advisers have been with other presidents. Byrnes was his own man and demanded the freedom to operate that way. This method of operating inevitably ran into conflict with Truman's strong views on the prerogatives of the President. It must also be remembered that Byrnes was considerably senior to Truman in the Democratic party. Although I never heard him mention the subject, Byrnes felt that he and not Truman should have been chosen by Roosevelt as the vice-presidential candidate in 1944. Under such circumstances, Byrnes believed that he held an independent position as Secretary of State.[52]

Whether consciously or not, Byrnes, in fact, preferred to pursue a policy he could manage on his own, with a small intimate team, to one in which he had to engage actively with the president. And it must have been hard for him to forget that Truman had promised to nominate him at the 1944 Democratic convention for the post of vice-president, a promise broken only at the strong, direct intervention of Roosevelt. I, at least, find it impossible to assess whether or to what extent these real enough elements of working style and personality played a part in the story.

But is it likely that, if the proposition were put to him by a united team, including Byrnes, Acheson, and Clayton, Truman would have reacted positively and been able to pull it off, including the mobilization of the requisite public and Senate support? On a matter of this kind, only tentative speculation is possible.

I would guess that Truman would have reacted positively. That was his instinct when large issues were clearly laid before him. He had great respect for Acheson and Clayton, with whom he worked well in the long intervals when Byrnes was out of town. A presentation uniting them with Byrnes would have impressed Truman. The all-European proposal, in its constructive dimensions, would have also appealed in part to the liberal wing of the Democratic party and eased Truman's political problem, much as the Marshall Plan did a year later. Moreover, Vandenberg, already a supporter of a long-run U.S. commitment to a German disarmament treaty, was troubled about Poland and Eastern Europe, about the possible split of Europe, and about the fate of the United Nations should the split come about.[53] After all, there is a sense in which, by reversing Lodge's role in relation to Wilson, the United Nations was Vandenberg's baby.

On the other hand, the gathering crisis of 1946 was less vivid and concrete than the threats to Greece and Turkey in March 1947, and the situation of the European economy was not quite as acute as it was to be in the winter of 1946–47. In his memoirs Jean Monnet observes: ". . . people only accept change when they are faced with necessity, and only recognize necessity when a crisis is upon them."[54] It can be argued, then, that, even if Byrnes and his colleagues had put the issue to Truman, either he or the country would have failed to respond because the crisis was not sufficient to cause an alteration in course.

For what it's worth, however, I conclude, on balance, that it is likely that if the Acheson-Clayton plan had been put to Truman, with Byrnes' support, he would have approved it; Vandenberg would have gone along; and the effort would have been made. Public opinion polls, as 1946 evolved, suggest that strong nonmilitary action by the United States may well have found public support. For example, a poll of September 18, 1946 (reported in *Public Opinion Quarterly*, Winter 1946–47), showed that 62 percent of Americans felt "less friendly" toward the Soviet Union than a year earlier; but 72 percent concluded that on October 10, 1946, existing disagreements did not justify going to war. A poll taken three days later indicated that 76 percent wanted the United States to be "fair but firm," telling the Soviet Union "just where we stand." But the simple fact is that the American political process proved capable of designing a policy toward Europe on these solid foundations in public opinion only in the face of the stark choices of the winter and spring of 1947.

The larger question, of course, is whether the outcome for Europe would have been significantly different if Truman had put the choice of Continental unity or a schism before Stalin in 1946, in the terms proposed by Acheson and Clayton, rather than in the context of the Truman Doctrine and the Marshall Plan a year later.

Three aspects of the situation would have been more propitious in 1946:

The June 1946 plebiscite in Poland, which Mikolajczyk clearly won, suggests the possibility, at least, that Soviet policy on Poland was still fluid. The continuing elements of democracy in Czechoslovakia and Hungary argue in the same direction. As late as October 1946, Moscow acquiesced in an election in Berlin in which the Communist-dominated Socialist Unity party (SED) received only 20 percent of the votes despite strong support from the occupation authorities in the Soviet Zone. By the summer of 1947, the Communists were much closer to total power in Poland and Hungary.

The situation in the Control Council in Berlin in the spring of 1946 suggests similarly that Stalin may not have yet made up his mind on an all-German settlement;[55] and he was, as the Berlin election suggests, less locked in to the notion of a Soviet-dominated East Germany.

Finally, if Truman had succeeded in rallying political support for the package as a whole, the image of progressive U.S. withdrawal from Europe in the minds of the Soviet leadership might have been reversed.

On the other hand, Stalin may still have opted for a split. It can be argued that most of the elements in the Acheson-Clayton proposal were, in fact, put to Moscow piecemeal in the course of 1946 and 1947: reparations from western Germany versus all-German institutions; a linking of the Western zones versus German unity; a disarmed Germany if it were unified; and, then, the Marshall Plan offer to Europe to the Urals, with its clear implication of economic aid for the Soviet Union.[56] In each case, Stalin rejected the larger American vision. It may be that, even rolled into a package, Stalin's answer in 1946 would have been the same one that emerged from the process that unrolled from, say, the breakdown of the Control Council in Berlin over reparations in May 1946, to Molotov's leaving the Marshall Plan conference in Paris in July 1947.

And, if the argument is correct that runs through this essay about the critical importance of Poland, it may be that only an American posture as serious, say, as that Truman was to mount with respect to Soviet withdrawal from Iran would have worked; the "whole hog" approach Kennan judged would be required to reverse the Soviet course in Eastern Europe (see above, p. 40). Here the evidence is reasonably clear. Neither after the First World War nor after the Second did the United States, through its political process, judge Eastern Europe a strategic area of importance sufficient to risk military action. Despite the American role in bringing independence to the Eastern European states, the United States never raised a finger during the interwar years significantly to support their survival. And, despite the intensity of Roosevelt's effort for a democratic Poland at Yalta and his concern down to the eve of his death, the State Department briefing book for Yalta may have been nearer the truth:

Briefing Book Paper: RECONSTRUCTION OF POLAND AND THE
    BALKANS: AMERICAN INTERESTS AND
    SOVIET ATTITUDE
1. Interests of the United States: political
. . . it now seems clear that the Soviet Union will exert predominant political influence over the areas in question. While this Government probably would not want to oppose itself to such a political configuration, neither would it desire to see American influence in this part of the world completely nullified.[57]

Even more significant is this comment of Vandenberg's as the potential Communist take-over of Poland became clear in the wake of Yalta:

> The desperately important question now is "what can we do about it?" Manifestly America will not go to war with Russia to settle such an issue—particularly when the President of the United States has endorsed the settlement. In the final analysis, we could not afford to upset our postwar peace plans on account of this issue. Yet I do not want to surrender to this decision insofar as we have any practical means at our disposal to continue to fight it. It seems to me that the best *practical* hope remaining to us is in my proposal that the new Peace League shall have a right to review all these interim decisions.[58]

The fact is that the United States has reacted with military conviction only when the balance of power in Europe or Asia was believed to be immediately at stake or to resist the military penetration of the hemisphere by a major potentially hostile power. The acquisition of Eastern Europe by the Soviet Union still left the balance of power in Europe in the hands of the West if it could organize itself to hold it. In 1945 and 1946 and subsequently, the United States and the other Western powers systematically drew back from the use of force or the threat of its use to enforce agreements or otherwise protect their interests in Eastern Europe.

Finally, there is Stalin's style itself. His whole history, within the Soviet Union as well as on the world scene, suggests that he was a man with a compulsion to exercise total power and that he preferred to exercise total power over a limited range rather than dilute power over a wider range. His successors, seeking to project Soviet power further out into the world, have had to live with more ambiguous and dilute situations, even in Eastern Europe. And even Stalin settled for a politically democratic, if unthreatening, Finland. But, when we cast up the accounts and identify the possible factors at work, Stalin's compulsions deserve to be taken into account.

Would anything short of the threat of using military force have preserved political democracy in Poland and Eastern Europe? To come to even a moderately confident answer to this question, one would require access to Soviet archives reflecting the inner debates of this period, for surely the various dimensions of the problem of European unity or schism were debated. It was no small thing for a Russian government to turn down an offer of long-term German disarmament, which Russians could help monitor, or even to refuse the offer for substantial aid in reconstruction implicit in the initial presentation of the Marshall Plan. The latter issue we know was intensively debated in Moscow.[59] Evidently, alternate objectives judged to be of higher priority tipped the balance. What they were and their relative weight we may never know.

On balance, I am less confident that even a maximum effort by the United States in 1946, short of military threat or action, could have avoided the split of Europe than I am that Truman would have accepted the Acheson-Clayton plan if laid before him; but it should not be forgotten that Moscow's decision to form an Eastern bloc, like the parallel process in the West, was arrived at only by a process taking place over time—a process Clay captures rather well for the period 1945 and 1946:

> At the time of the Potsdam Conference our strength in Europe was at its peak. Our armies were deep in Germany, Austria, and Czechoslovakia. The extent of our air and armored power was evident everywhere. New governments in Poland, Czechoslovakia, and Hungary had Communist participation, but were not Communist-dominated. Even the Balkan States were not under Communist control and Generalissimo Stalin was not sure that it could be imposed in these countries. Hence, at Potsdam, the Soviet representatives had been willing to accept a unified Germany under quadripartite control and to depend on open Communist political action to dominate its life, since the Communist

party in Germany was recognized as a democratic party. Open and underground political activities would be undertaken elsewhere to implant Communism throughout Europe. Meanwhile the Soviet economy would be restored in part with German capital equipment and the pent-up consumer demand satisfied as much as possible with German productive output. If Germany ended in economic chaos it would be even more susceptible to Communist indoctrination. . . .

I do not believe that either in Potsdam or in the Paris conferences the Soviet Government had a definite, long-range plan in mind. Its policy of Communist world domination which had been checked by war was brought out of moth balls and clearly formed the basis of their day-to-day planning, which was still, however, on an expediency basis.

In the spring of 1946 the situation in Europe had changed materially. Our forces had been withdrawn from Czechoslovakia and were contained in our occupation areas in Germany and Austria. While the process of redeployment still left us with a larger force in Europe than we were to have later, it was no longer the powerful military organization with which we had ended the war. Communist control of the eastern European countries was becoming stronger each day and its penetration into western Europe was gaining momentum, but even with these gains the Soviet position was not yet sufficiently entrenched to permit the clanging of the Iron Curtain. . . .[60]

The existence of this possible uncertainty in Soviet policy as of the spring and summer of 1946 leaves the third question posed in this chapter open—but, on present evidence, unanswerable. Although I still regret that the Acheson-Clayton plan was not carried forward to execution in 1946, I would, of course, not assert that such an effort would certainly have avoided the split of Europe and thus avoided the Cold War as we have known it. A part of my regret centers on the judgment, in retrospect, that we in GA were correct on one issue: it was a major technical diplomatic error to concentrate in 1946 on the peripheral treaties and leave the critical issue of

Germany to the Control Council test. Patricia Ward has put that judgment as follows:

> Also handicapping the Council of Foreign Ministers was the Potsdam decision to begin first with the lesser treaties and then to deal with Austria and Germany. Bidault said, "The troubles of the war-shattered world are like a tangled skein. The threads have to be straightened out; but this cannot be done by pulling at the end of one thread after another. The skein is full of knots, and the main knot is Germany." Germany was not just a French obsession; Nicolson wrote, "To approach this central problem tentatively, and from the easiest end, was to be stung by each of the nettles without firmly grasping a single one." Since American-Soviet confrontation over the peace settlement had to come, it was better to have it over Germany immediately, because a settlement there would be of more value than one on the lesser treaties. Discussing Germany first might have led to a general European settlement, a frank acknowledgment of existing spheres of influence and, if not the avoidance, at least the easing, of a Soviet-American encounter. Certainly beginning with Germany would have strengthened the American-British position because they controlled two-thirds of Germany and their military power was there, not in Eastern Europe. Since the Soviet strength was in Eastern Europe, all Byrnes could do was protest and criticize and by so doing, estrange the Soviets. Pointing this out in an article summarizing the work of the council, the American journalist, Walter Lippmann, characterized the decision to begin with satellite treaties "a gigantic blunder," which challenged the Russians "first of all on the ground where they were most able to be, and were most certain to be, brutal, stubborn, faithless and aggressive." [61]

Byrnes, in effect, responded to Ward's argument in his *Speaking Frankly*:

> Sincere and well-intentioned people have held the view that the German problem should have been settled first. Virtually everything that has happened since the end of the

war has confirmed in my mind the wisdom of concluding the lesser treaties first. The record of those negotiations amply demonstrates the ingenuity of the Soviet delegation at bargaining and log rolling in the pursuit of their objectives; it illustrates their willingness to block agreement on a non-controversial, universally accepted proposal in order to obtain concessions on some wholly unrelated issue they consider important. Such tactics would have had free play if all the complex problems of the German and Austrian settlements had been added to those of the five lesser treaties. The restoration of peace in any area would have been delayed for years to come.[62]

What Byrnes' argument fails to take into account is the deterioration of prospects for an all-German settlement in the course of 1946 and the extent to which the American posture on the peripheral treaties and acquiescence in the Communist take-over of Poland helped strengthen the case in Moscow for a split Germany by 1947.

Behind Byrnes' acquiescence in delaying the approach to a German settlement were, of course, all the factors evoked earlier bearing on the setting of the U.S. posture in 1946, including the apprehension or judgment in the Foreign Service that a split Germany and Europe was the optimum outcome obtainable. Still, I believe, the test would have been sounder if, at the highest level, the United States had insisted after Potsdam that the German issue be confronted; and, if that were done, the logic of the situation and the diverse interests in play would have required that the German negotiation be framed by something like the Acheson-Clayton proposal. To revert to Joseph Jones' dictum (see above, p. 74), that proposal, a year before Marshall's negotiations in Moscow, did respect the fact that "to deal with the problem of Germany it was necessary to deal with the problem of Europe."

As of 1981, men in both Moscow and the Western capitals might conclude that, given human imperfections and the sweep of European history, the actual outcome has been tolerably satisfactory.[63] There has been no war in Europe for thirty-five years. The Berlin crises of 1948 to 1949 and 1961 to 1962 were weathered without escalation as well as the crises in Czechoslovakia (1948 and 1968), East Germany (1953), Poland and Hungary (1956), and, down to this writing, Poland again (1980 to 1981). Eastern, as well as Western Europe, has achieved substantial economic and social progress. Some of the ties of culture and trade that for so long bound Eastern and Western Europe over the centuries have been revived. The capacity of the United States to maintain substantial forces in Western Europe has proved to be greater than I, at least, thought likely in 1946 and the Atlantic Alliance as a whole sturdier. Similarly, the German people have accepted the division of their country with more grace than many then supposed would prove possible, although the impulse for unity remains beneath the surface. But the demeaning human costs of Soviet domination in Eastern Europe have been high; the massive confrontation of nuclear and conventional forces down the center of Europe has been expensive and its long-run stability not guaranteed; and it still remains to be seen if Stalin's "confederation" in Eastern Europe will provide long-run security or progressively heightened insecurity for the Soviet peoples. And if, as seems wholly possible, the abiding nationalism and rising desire for human freedom in Eastern Europe yield in the times ahead a crisis beyond the Soviet capacity to manage, the West may yet have to offer something like the Acheson-Clayton proposal as an alternative to cataclysm.

Putting aside these not very fruitful counterfactual speculations, there are, I believe, two elements incorporated in this essay which deserve greater weight than they are usually given in the lively, contentious literature on the origins of the Cold War.

First, the somewhat neglected year, 1946, justifies more

attention than it is accorded.[64] The three dramatic events of 1947—the Truman Doctrine, Marshall's frustration in Moscow on the German issue, and the negative Soviet posture on the Marshall Plan in Paris—emerge as the climax to a year of relatively quiet but progressive deterioration in U.S.-Soviet relations. The Cold War appears to crystallize as the result of an incremental, interacting process rather than as a purposeful clash of wills and lucid strategies.

Second, to the extent that the United States bears responsibility for the emergence of the Cold War in Europe, that responsibility flows not from its overbearing challenge to vital Soviet interests but from its weak and defensive stance, framed not only by the unilateral dismantling of the armed forces but also by a doubt of our capacity to sustain an effective presence in Europe for the long pull. That doubt suffused the perspectives and policies of the Soviet, British, and French governments. Andrei Y. Vishinsky is reported to have once told an American citizen that the United States deceived the Soviet Union in Korea. And he had a case. It was not easy to guess, from the withdrawal of U.S. forces from South Korea, the inadequate U.S. forces positioned in Japan, the enunciation of a U.S. defense perimeter in the Pacific that failed to include South Korea, that the United States would fight a considerable war in its defense. Somewhat similarly, there was nothing in the U.S. diplomatic performance in 1946 that permitted the Soviet authorities to predict the Truman Doctrine, the Marshall Plan, NATO, SHAPE, and the presence of substantial U.S. forces in Europe thirty-six years after V-E Day. The Cold War may have been ultimately caused by a U.S. policy in 1946 that tempted Stalin with visions of a possible extension of Soviet power that no Russian or Communist ruler could, in good conscience, refuse to pursue.

But the most fundamental and abiding lesson illustrated by this story is that Soviet foreign policy for more than thirty-five years has been substantially determined by Moscow's perception of U.S. capabilities, determination, and will. Over this era one could never ask, "What are Soviet intentions?" without simultaneously answering the question, "What is the Soviet view of the United States?"

Appendix A

Three Versions of the Proposal
for an All-European Settlement

[*Note*: Following are three versions of the proposal ultimately laid before Byrnes by Acheson and Clayton on April 20, 1946. The first is, I believe, the initial formulation of the proposal including a discussion of the possible arguments against it. The second, accompanied by the memoranda of Emilio Collado, Clayton's aide, is dated February 25, 1946, and moved forward the next day. The third was drafted in April in a form which might, after refinement, have been laid by Byrnes before the Foreign Ministers in Paris.]

Version 1

DRAFT OF PROPOSED
U.S. PLAN FOR A EUROPEAN SETTLEMENT: SPRING 1946

I. *Aim*

The purpose of the following outline proposals is to check the tendency towards the formation of exclusive blocs in Europe, and to provide a framework of major power accord within which Europe might peacefully recover and develop an increasing measure of unity over the coming years. To execute these proposals requires that the United States bring the full weight of its diplomatic power and bargaining position to bear. The proposals are consistent with the principles of the UNO Charter. They require, however, some extension of the UNO Structure.

II. *Present Position*

These proposals are based on an analysis which regards the following factors as basic to the present position:

A. The re-emergence of USSR after forty years of military defeat, revolution, and repression within its own borders, as a major power in East and South-East Europe;

B. Failure of Yalta, Potsdam, and UNO to provide adequate machinery in Europe capable of preventing the split of Europe into relatively exclusive East and West blocs;

C. Judgment by the governments of USSR, U.K., and France that the positive interest of the US in the structure of Europe was likely to prove transitory;

D. United States policy which has thus far prevented the split of Europe, but which has not halted the tendency in that direction.

III. *U.S. Plan: Summary*

In brief the proposed United States approach would consist of the simultaneous presentation of:

A. Plan, involving extension of UNO structure, to provide machinery for Continent-wide consultation on a specific range of issues, within a framework of major power accord;

B. Formulae, consistent with such a plan, for settling the range of major outstanding issues of diplomatic conflict in Europe.

This approach is based on a judgment that, until the question of whether Europe shall split in the near future is decided, the settlement of particular questions will prove virtually impossible. The presentation of A and B above, might well be accompanied by public assertion of the following:

1. The continuing and direct U.S. security stake in the structure and stability of Europe, in the light of U.S. involvement in two European wars, and the development of new military weapons;

2. U.S. opposition to an exclusive bloc structure for Europe as unstable, dangerous, and corrosive to all the larger conceptions on which we have all agreed;

3. U.S. belief that tendency towards unilateral and regional actions incompatible with development of UNO must be halted, by extended exploration, of U.S. proposals A and B, above;

4. U.S. faith that if problems frankly faced and discussed—with strong assertion of U.S. interest—that a framework of major power accord for Europe can be found.

IV. *Plan for European UNO Machinery*

The following outline plan would be related, structurally, to the appropriate branches of the UNO. It would constitute an extension of the central organization, but would be so organized as to avoid violating its basic unity. (Appendix required on structural details of organization, to be done by United States experts on UNO.)

It is judged necessary that provision be made for treatment of European problems at two levels: an assembly level which would seek agreement on technical issues on a majority basis of some agreed kind; and a Security Council level where the security interests of the major powers might intervene. In general it would be hoped that the presence at the Assembly level of major-power non-voting, but active observers would serve to achieve solutions agreeable to the major powers, and thus minimize the issues which might be formally brought to the Security Council for settlement.

Assembly Level

The Assembly would consist simply of sub-committees, empowered to deal with a specified range of particular problems on a Continent-wide basis. Each member would have a single vote; and a majority (or perhaps ⅔) vote would prevail. Voting membership would include all members of the United Nations in Europe, excluding U.K. and U.S.S.R. These latter powers and the U.S. would fully participate in the meetings on a non-voting basis. U.S.S.R. might insist on the membership of the Ukraine and the Byelo-Russian Republics, which might well be accepted, so long as majority (or ⅔) rule were maintained. The range of issues to be dealt with, and the terms of reference within which the Assembly organizations would be empowered to act would be set by the Security Council of the United Nations. A possible range of initial organizations within the assembly would be the following:

1. Fuel and Power (Appendix required of LA/Stillwell, Jackson): This would involve an extension of the ECO, both with respect to membership, and to include issues connected with electric power distribution.
2. Trade: (Appendix required of CP) involving extension of EECE, acting as clearing house for trade agreements, and efforts to set up common trade policies for Europe in conformity with general ECOSOC principles.

3. Transport: (Appendix required of TRC) involving extension of scope of ECITO, with special role as guardian of common European policies on freedom of navigation for waterways.

4. Finance: (Appendix required of FN, in conjunction with Bretton Woods Fund officials) involving measures for stabilizing European currencies, common European measures to combat inflation, looking towards development of a common Continental currency, related to dollar.

5. Planning: (Appendix required of ED, in conjunction with Bretton Woods bank officials) involving coordination of capital development plans, including distribution of capacity removed from Germany as reparations; possibility of Danubian TVA, etc.

Other economic branches can easily be envisaged, as well as political branches dealing with such problems as Displaced Persons, uniformity of passport regulations, etc. The present list is illustrative, and is believed to be within the range of prompt negotiation and implementation.

Security Council Level

In addition to the ties which the organization within the Assembly would have with ECOSOC, Bretton Woods, and other worldwide organizations, direct screening of basic decisions, and definition of terms of reference would be reserved to the Security Council. Over a period of time it would be the hope that, as confidence grew, the range of issues and authority permitted the Assembly organizations would expand; and that the area of security intervention on the part of the Great Powers would contract. Voting procedures at this level would follow normal Security Council UNO procedures.

V. *Formulae for Settlement Outstanding Issues*

It is evident that, while acceptance of machinery of this type would facilitate negotiation of many particular current issues, a European settlement must include specific provision for their solution. The following are possible formulae for some of the major current European problems, consistent with the assumption that Major Power accord in Europe will continue.

1. Rhineland-Ruhr: Political separation avoided with some limited

	concessions to French view (see EUR-ESP-ORI paper).
2. Danube:	Riparian states only on permanent commission, with symmetrical arrangement for Rhine and other international European rivers; freedom of navigation guaranteed by European transport organization above.
3. Germany:	Proceed promptly with Potsdam, reparations, central agencies, reactivation German economy.
4. Austria:	Prompt settlement German assets issues, leaving some USSR ownership confined if possible to oil, and shipping on Danube; but no extra-territorial status for such ownership; proceed with Austrian treaty; entrance Austria to UNO and withdrawal of troops.
5. East Europe:	Consolidation, and if possible, reduction USSR reparations out of current output; no extra-territorial status Russian ownership rights; U.S. recovery aid.
6. Mediterranean:	The issues of Dardanelles, Turkey, and USSR relation to Middle East oil must be faced, probably, if this plan is to prove acceptable.

In general forcing of quadripartite forum extension represents weakening of most aggressive USSR elements, and threat to USSR of an independent Continent or growing independence; and short-run compensatory concessions might well be required.

VI. *Possible Objections*

There are a number of just and obvious queries to be made of the line of policy indicated above.

a) *International accord is not achieved by mechanisms, but from the outlook and spirit of the powers engaged in negotiation.* This judgment is clearly applicable. In the first instance, there can be little doubt that a European Organization would merely transfer to a new forum the present struggle for national power and influence. It would have initially only the advantage of promising that such struggle take place within a framework of international organization rather than as between virtually autonomous blocs. Over a longer period it holds the possibility that the measure of independence allowed the smaller European countries will expand, and that the intervention of the Great Powers will be confined to a narrowing range of problems affecting large questions of security.

b) *The UNO Assembly and Security Council already exist.* The machinery now in prospect within the UNO does not appear to offer a forum for the continuous issues of European housekeeping and national interplay. In any case, the fact that blocs are now rapidly in the process of emergence simultaneously with the development of UNO machinery, indicates *prima facie* the need for some additional structure.

c) *U.S. efforts to maintain major power accord have already indicated the impossibility of altering the unilateral basis on which the USSR is proceeding in Europe.* The weight attached to this judgment depends largely on whether it is believed that USSR is acting on the assumption of future diminished U.S. concern in European affairs. USSR response to the alternatives of a European Organization or vigorous US support for a Western bloc cannot fairly be pre-judged. In addition it is to be noted that, despite firm insistence on certain minimum unilateral controls over the countries of Eastern Europe, USSR policy has varied widely, as between, say, Finland, and Bulgaria; Czechoslovakia and Hungary. The possibility that the USSR might ultimately permit, with certain security guarantees, the participation of Eastern European countries in a European organization can, on present evidence, by no means be excluded.

d) *USSR might make the European Organization a vehicle for attempted extension of Soviet influence.* It is undeniable that this will be the case. Similarly it is clear that the Western powers will attempt to extend their influence through such an organization. Conflict of political conception and of national or regional interest cannot, of course, be avoided by any organization, even if it were intrinsically desirable. The advantage of a European organization is that it offers the possibility of bringing the inevitable conflicts of East and West Europe within the orbit of rules of law; and of offering to the more than 300 million people between the English Channel and the Curzon line an enlarging voice in their own affairs and a position somewhat more independent than at present of the security objectives of the major powers.

e) *The French might insist that such a scheme does not provide sufficient direct checks on the influence and power of a unified Germany.* It is known that the Socialist Party has only reluctantly accepted the French Government's Rhineland-Ruhr proposals, and that it has, in principle, opposed the dismemberment of Germany. The Communist Party has supported the Rhineland-Ruhr proposal with the reservation that the area not be subject to exclusively Western Control. An effective re-assertion of Big Three accord, in the terms suggested above, might well remove much of the ground from the French Government's position. In addition, the following special limitations on Germany's relative power in Europe are contemplated under Potsdam, or might well be considered.

1. Sharp initial reduction in Germany's post-war economic strength;
2. relatively more rapid recovery and economic expansion in France and elsewhere on Continent, due to reparations and U.S. loans;
3. permanent French acquisition of Saar;
4. ownership of Ruhr coal, iron and steel industries by European organization;
5. explicit guarantees against re-armament in German Treaty; with perhaps other limitations on German sovereignty;
6. opportunity for France to assume role of leadership, on Continent-wide basis, within European Organization.

f) *U.S. initiative in pressing for such a European solution may fail.* The nature of the alternative to a European Organization, which is discussed below, makes it desirable in the U.S. interest to press for the superior solution, however small the chances of success may initially appear to be. Only after exhaustion of the line of approach it represents does acceptance of a bloc alternative appear justified.

VII. *The Alternative*

The principal alternative to the re-establishment of major power accord in Europe is the formation of relatively exclusive blocs. The formation of such blocs, or the assumption that they will form, constitutes the basis of USSR, U.K., and French policy in Europe. From the point of view of the West this is a policy frankly of despair, disruptive of every enunciated conception of U.S. political and economic foreign policy. It is doubtful, further, whether it will lead to a condition of even temporary stability in Europe.

In particular, crystallization of exclusive blocs would appear to involve the following:

a) the association of German sentiment for unity with the more aggressive of the two blocs, almost certainly the East;
b) intensification of efforts by each bloc to foster and maintain minority elements within the other bloc;
c) development of the blocs toward military coalition, engaged in active armaments competition.

In such a situation the Western Powers, due to the inhibitions within their political life, would be at a distinct disadvantage; and a progressive extension of the Eastern sphere would be anticipated.

From the outset the United States would be confronted with very strong pressures to support, economically and militarily, the Western bloc. Confronted with the choice of supporting such a bloc, or retiring to isolation, it is doubtful over a period of time whether popular sentiment in the U.S. would accept the former course, especially if the USSR were content to use means short of overt military action to secure its end. In short, it appears to be the main hope for the maintenance and extension of Western concepts and Western political power, that the structure of negotiation be elaborated to deal with an expanding range of issues, in Europe as elsewhere.

Version 2

DATE: Feb. 26, 1946

TO: A-C—Mr. Clayton
FROM: A-C/F—Mr. Collado

I should like to talk to you about the material contained in the attached memoranda which present a point of view which I have discussed with you on several occasions. I think the general line is right. I think it could be presented more forcefully, but I am not sure that the specific program outlined in the attachments is fully adequate.

DATE: February 25, 1946

TO: AC—Mr. Clayton
FROM: AC/F—E. G. Collado
SUBJECT: *U.S. Foreign Policy Toward Europe and Its Economic Implications*

ESP and OFD are currently encountering obstacles in the conduct of their affairs due to apparent lack of basic agreement in the Department as to an appropriate consistent overall United States policy toward Europe, and the relations of the Soviet Union to Europe. I would suggest the situation calls for:

a) Clarification of policy within the Department;
b) Approach to the governments of the other major powers on the basis of a wide range of issues.

From the perspective of economic policy it appears that a general European Treaty may prove a pre-requisite to settlement of many particular outstanding issues.

The loan program, the disposal of surplus property, the economic features of United States policy in Germany and Austria, including reparation, restitution, levels of industry, etc., the protection of foreign investment abroad, along with a number of other issues in ITP and TRC on which I am partially informed, are either totally stalled, or are making progress only on a limited atomistic basis. Each action taken in these fields involves a renewed and temporary resolution in the Department of differences as to appropriate overall policy toward Europe; and the extent of progress is severely limited by ambiguities, shared by all the major powers, surrounding the shape of Europe over the coming years. The major strands of thought which must be resolved recurrently, within the Department as issues arise may be characterized as follows:

a) *Prevention of a split between Eastern and Western Europe*
If this be United States policy in Europe, it would appear to call for action by the United States as a mediator between Eastern and Western Europe, much as General Clay has served as a mediator in the Allied Control Council for Germany. Em-

phasis would be on an independent interpretation of United States obligations and commitments in Europe, without reference to Eastern or Western interpretations prior to negotiation, and on continuous efforts to obtain agreements on treaties, interpretation of property rights, economic and political penetration, etc.

b) *The defense of Western Europe against Eastern Europe*
There is some disposition in the Department to regard the split of Europe between East and West as a foregone conclusion, and to prepare to support the Western Bloc of Europe against the East. This position is believed to be the inescapable conclusion of those who think that it is possible to deal with Eastern Europe but only on a tough bargaining basis of quid-pro-quos. (see c, below)

c) *Bargain with the Soviet Union over Europe*
If the Soviet Union lives up to its commitments only when it suits her to do so, as is widely alleged in the Department, there is room for making all responses to our own commitments and obligations conditional on specific quid-pro-quos from the Soviet Union involving its commitments. It is recommended, for example, that the United States delay further progress in the German reparation settlement until the Soviet Union lives up more fully to the political principles of the Potsdam Protocol; that our loan policy discriminate obviously among countries in Eastern Europe according to their efforts to retain a Western orientation; that we withhold restitution of Jugoslav barges looted by the Nazis and now in our possession in Austria and Germany until Jugoslavia gives us a concession on the treatment of American property owners in the current nationalization program.

In my judgement, recent Russian action in Eastern Europe and the Stalin speech has made it desirable to come to a new understanding with the Soviet Union as to their power role in Europe. Basically, this requires agreed decision as to whether European blocs should be de-limited and crystallized, or whether we shall form a structure for Europe as a whole, with continued negotiation of outstanding issues. If this is not done, foreign lending, surplus property, occupation, property, transportation and similar economic policy in Europe will continue to rest on the uneasy basis of underlying conflict in the Department among the various types of policy toward Europe which might be pursued. Such an understanding could be reached by offering the Soviet Union a choice between a renewed understanding or a split in Europe, under the latter of which the United States would veto all loans to Eastern Europe, UNRRA for the USSR and Eastern Europe, sales of surplus property, recapture of lend-lease property, vigorous defense of property rights, withholding of reparation due Eastern Europe under the Potsdam agreement, etc. As a constructive step toward the former, I attach a memorandum for purposes of discussion, prepared in draft by a member of GA, suggesting the basis for a wide area of agreement in Europe among the major powers.

I submit that the policy of bargaining specific issues out against one another, outlined in *c* above, is undesirable. In my judgement it will accomplish little toward satisfaction of U.S. or other national interests and will rapidly culminate in a split of Europe into blocs.

Should you consider the suggestion in the attached memorandum worthy of consideration in the Department—it has had no criticism as yet from Mr. Dunn's staff—you may wish to submit it to the Secretary's staff committee for its consideration.

GA:C. P. Kindleberger:shp   ESP   OFD

DRAFT

U.S. POLICY AND THE PROBLEM OF EUROPEAN BLOCS

1. *The Problem*

It has become increasingly clear since V-E day that strong forces are at work tending to split Europe into two exclusive antagonistic blocs. This tendency arises largely from the re-emergence of Russia as a major power in Eastern and Central Europe, the diplomatic actions that have accompanied its re-emergence, and the fears engendered by those actions in the countries of Western Europe. The possibility that at some time in the not-distant future present tensions may crystallize into clear cut blocs itself strengthens the forces making for such blocs; for on each side there is a reluctance to make concessions, necessary in the general interest, which might weaken the strength, diminish the scope, or corrupt the coherence of a future bloc.

The fission of Europe would be inherently unstable and would, therefore, not be in the American interest. It would lead, inevitably, to the suppression of opposition within each bloc, and to the forcing of economic and political life into an exclusive pattern. It would strike at the root conception of the U.N.O. as well as at the whole framework of U.S. international economic policy. It would almost certainly lead to an armaments race on a very large scale.

In the sequence of military and diplomatic arrangements that began with the German attack on U.S.S.R. in June 1941, the U.S. has consistently stood for a conception of the European war and the peace which regarded Europe as a whole; although that conception recognized within the framework of Europe the existence of legitimate national and regional interests. Since Potsdam United States influence has been, in general, directed to the maintenance and extension of such quadripartite elements as were incorporated in the Berlin Agreement; and to a resolution of existing unilateral arrangements which would be consistent with a long run unified structure for Europe as a whole.

The role of the United States in relation to the Three main European Powers in the months since V-E Day appears to indicate that the European policy of United States may well decide whether the split in Europe will take place. The operation of the Control Council, Germany, would for example almost certainly have broken down, and Germany split into two segments without the presence of the United States' element, and the policy position it has consistently assumed.

The emergence of issues, such as the Balkan Peace Treaties and the Rhineland-Ruhr question, which patently concern the long run shape of Europe, and the occurrence of indications within U.S. life and policy which many Europeans have taken to presage a withdrawal of U.S. from European affairs have sharpened the issue of whether Europe shall split, and they have on the whole strengthened the forces making for virtually independent blocs. These facts make urgent the formulation of a clear U.S. policy for Europe. An ambiguous American policy or one infirmly executed is likely to prove tantamount to support for the formation of blocs.

Any policy designed to yield a unified structure for Europe must take account of and resolve the following basic forces:

1. The security interests of USSR;

2. The natural regional ties among the countries of Eastern Europe;
3. The security interests of U.K. and of France;
4. The natural regional ties among the countries of Western Europe;
5. The diverse, unique interests of the various individual countries of Europe.

It must also be a policy which, while defining a large long range goal for Europe, is at the same time capable of informing current day to day issues of policy.

2. *Recommendations*

A. The Department make public on the highest level its concern over the tendency towards blocs in Europe, and its advocacy of an alternative solution. Draft of a proposed statement of this general character is attached.

B. Each division of the Department concerned with aspects of European political and economic affairs be requested to survey the current main issues with which it is now dealing, to state present Department policy on those issues and its relation to the problem of East and West European blocs.

C. A committee be set up within the Department:

a) to survey current policy on particular issues affecting the problem of blocs, including replies under B, above;

b) to make recommendations to the Secretary designed to increase the consistency and improve the effectiveness of current U.S. policy in Europe;

c) to formulate immediately a plan for the organization of Europe within the UNO which would meet the long run objectives of U.S. policy. A brief outline of such a plan is attached. It is envisaged that a plan of this character be presented by the United States member, at the next meeting of the Foreign Secretaries.

DRAFT

UNITED STATES POLICY FOR EUROPE
Proposed Public Statement

As a natural outgrowth of the European war, and of the arrangements that have grown up in the post-war months, there has arisen in Europe a tendency towards the formation of exclusive Eastern and Western blocs. It is the policy of the United States to oppose the formation of such blocs, because it believes they would lead to the repression of individual and national liberties, to large scale competition in armaments, and to the danger of war.

In executing this policy the United States, while recognizing the existence of legitimate national and regional interests, has supported strongly such quadripartite organizations as the Control Council, Germany, and the Allied Council, Austria. More broadly, in UNRRA and the various emergency economic organizations now dealing with European reconstruction problems, this government has accepted the concept of a European community and has worked for the extension of its scope.

For the immediate future the United States Government will continue to press for the maintenance and strengthening of those institutions and procedures which provide for consultation and negotiation among all the powers concerned with European problems; and within them we will jointly seek solutions to current problems and controversies. Such solutions, while resolving conflicts of national and regional interest, should, in the United States view, be consistent with the gradual development of an organization for Europe as a whole.

Simultaneously, however, a larger approach to this problem is required. The settlement of particular issues is made difficult, and at times impossible by the doubt which exists as to the general shape of Europe's organization over the next decade and beyond. If Europe is to form into two relatively exclusive blocs, that likelihood has consequences for a host of particular questions which the powers are now attempting to resolve. If quadripartite consultation is to persist, and to broaden to permit a role for the smaller European states, acceptance of that probability will shape the resolution of these questions in a different direction. Therefore, the United States will immediately raise with the governments of France, U.K., and U.S.S.R. a proposal for a general European Organization, within the framework of the U.N.O. The United States government believes that such an organization alone holds promise of providing security to the countries of Europe, large and small, and to the rest of the world, which has a direct security interest in the maintenance of European peace. Given the present grave concern of the major powers for their future security, the development of a European organization will require time and patient negotiation. Acceptance in principle of a framework for Europe as a whole should, however, provide a setting within which outstanding particular issues may be rapidly settled.

DRAFT

OUTLINE PLAN FOR ORGANIZING
A EUROPEAN BRANCH OF U.N.O.

I. *General.* Any present proposal for an organization for Europe as a whole must have two characteristics:

    a) it must be accompanied by a proposed settlement in principle at least of a wide range of outstanding current issues;

    b) it must be defined with sufficient precision so that U.S.S.R. on the one hand, and the Western Powers on the other judge that it does not involve a worsening in their *relative* security positions, vis-a-vis one another.

In effect, condition b), above, requires that initially the organization deal with a limited range of issues, with fairly extensive checks on the subject matter and decisions of the proposed organization, by the major powers. Only gradually may it be expected that its scope and authority would widen. Initially it must be regarded as simply effecting a settlement of certain outstanding particular issues, and creating a potential forum for future problems.

The following memorandum briefly outlines:

    a) possible formulae for the settlement of particular outstanding issues;

    b) a possible outline of organizational structure;

    c) a possible initial range of agreed subject matter for treatment within such an organization.

II. *Outstanding Issues* (Following designed to be illustrative only).

    A. *Reparations out of Current Output.* U.S.S.R. agrees to make final its claims for reparations out of current output from East European countries, and to revise them in such a way as to be compatible with the reconstruction of such countries, and the prompt revival of normal patterns of international trade in that area. Report of results plus terms of trade treaties to European Foreign Trade Organization.

B. *Property Ownership.* Recognition of Allied Ownership interests in East Europe, and limitation by Forced Transfer Agreement of U.S.S.R. acquisitions under Potsdam. All foreign ownership interests to enjoy comparable status; such status to be compatible with economic sovereignty of each nation, except as limited by European Organization as a whole. Commissions to operate reporting to European Organization.

C. *Danube and Mediterranean.* Permanent control of Danube and Rhine to be settled on basis riparian states only, with surveillance by European Transport Organization. Dardanelles and Suez to be put under parallel international organization. Latter under surveillance of UNO.

D. *Germany.* Saar awarded to France. Ruhr industry under European Organization Corporation, but no economic or political detachment. Otherwise proceed with Potsdam, with immediate setting up Central Administrative Agencies.

E. *Austria.* Firm date for Treaty; immediate reduction of troops; settlement of German assets question, as under B, above.

F. *Spain.* Agreement to remove Franco from Spain, with provision for free election under UNO, covering choice of government and monarchy question.

G. *European Organization Membership.* All European countries join the European Organization (see III, below).

H. *U.S. Loan Policy.* United States grant loan ($1 billion) to U.S.S.R. and raise proposed level of loans to Jugoslavia and Poland.

III. *Outline Organizational Structure.*

A. *Security Council.*

Representatives of UNO Security Council, operating under normal voting procedures. Council empowered to enlarge or contract range of issues treated within Assembly and related organizations. Council required to pass on all substantive agreements reached in Assembly.

B. *Assembly.*

All European Countries ex-U.K. and U.S.S.R. one vote per country (or, say, votes proportional to population); majority vote (or, say, ⅔ majority). U.K., U.S.S.R., and U.S. to hold non-voting membership, as observers.

IV. *Related Organizations** (to be related to appropriate UNO categories)

1. Fuel
2. Foreign Trade
3. Transport
4. Finance
5. Long Term Planning: Disposition of Reparations and adjustment of national and regional capital development schemes.

*Economic organizations only cited here, for illustrative purposes.

GA: W. W. Rostow:shp 2/25/46

Version 3

UNITED STATES PROPOSALS
FOR A EUROPEAN SETTLEMENT

It is the view of the United States Government that a Europe fully recovered from war, settling its problems by common action, within democratic principles, is essential to the success of the United Nations, and to the peace of the world. It is the policy of the United States constructively to aid in the successive necessary steps in this evolution.

The United States Government is, however, deeply disturbed by the development in Europe of two interrelated tendencies: on the one hand a series of important subjects of negotiation in Europe have reached points of impasse among the Great Powers; on the other, increasing numbers of minor problems affecting the daily life of the European states are being treated as matters of major concern requiring intervention by the Great Powers—or are being neglected.

The United States deplores the failure to arrive at common understandings upon outstanding issues, and is conscious of the great difficulties which beset the countries of Europe, east and west, in sustaining and strengthening their economic and political life. The difficulties referred to arise from inevitable and proper differences of view on particular issues, but also from grave uncertainty concerning the extent of future cooperation in Europe among European and non-European states. The United States Government has noted with concern the development of comment on these questions which seems based on the assumption that Europe must one day divide into exclusive eastern and western "blocs". The United States Government considers that the security of Europe and therewith of the United States would be endangered by such a division of Europe and seeks to prevent such a division.

It is, therefore, the intention of the Secretary of State to explore fully with his colleagues on the occasion of these meetings the possibilities of a settlement that will provide for Europe a unified structure, within a continuing framework of quadripartite accord.

It is believed that the solution to the particular issues with which we are now confronted would be materially aided were the Council to agree to the immediate creation of certain specific organizations to be extended in future years into a strong continent-wide system of European consultation and collaboration. To these ends the Secretary of State proposes to his colleagues:

a) A concrete plan (Appendix A) for European collaboration on a specified wide range of economic issues as a supplement to the concerted and simultaneous effort to reach a settlement on the unresolved issues in the draft peace treaties, prepared by the Deputy Foreign Ministers.

b) Specific formulae (Appendix B) for the settlement of certain other particular questions with which we are not confronted. The plan (Appendix A) attached is designed to achieve two ends:

a) to achieve a reconciliation of the security interests of the Four powers without formation of relatively exclusive spheres of influence in Europe;

b) within that framework to permit and encourage maximum economic and political self-determination for the individual countries of Europe and maximum provision for cooperation in the solution of common technical and economic problems.

The plan provides for the setting up of a Council for Europe, to replace the Council of Foreign Ministers after the present session, which would deal with security issues which may arise in Europe. It provides further for the creation of a series of Commissions organized under a European Economic and Social Council, to be concerned with a range of technical problems, including development and distribution of fuel and power resources, and food supply. Provision is made in these Commissions for ultimate representation of all European countries. The framework of organization is so drawn as to be consistent with, and supplementary to the functions and activities of the United Nations.

The Charter of the United Nations provides explicitly for the possibility that regional organizations may develop. The need in Europe for such organizations is indicated by the development, in recent months, of the ECO, EECE, and ECITO. It is the view of the Secretary of State that such organizations should be extended uniformly, on agreed terms, on a continent-wide basis, and that they should be fully linked to the Economic and Social Council of the United Nations.

The Secretary of State appreciates that, in order to put into operation a plan such as that outlined above, it is necessary first to settle within the Council of Foreign Ministers certain particular outstanding issues, in relation to the treaties, and to our occupation of Germany and Austria. Specific formulae concerning the latter are suggested in Appendix B. The Secretary of State strongly urges upon his colleagues that in the spirit of our war-time alliance and our various common statements of post-war intentions, these matters be now approached in terms of settlements, consistent with the spirit and form of the type of European organization outlined above.

DRAFT   APPENDIX A   *SECRET*
Proposal for the Creation
of
Certain European Organizations.

In essence the United States proposes that, within a framework of major power accord and assistance, the European countries should be enabled and encouraged to work out the solution of their problems, free from fear of aggression or intervention by any power.

For this purpose the United States proposes two related European organizations:

1. A Council for Europe of which the Soviet Union, Great Britain, the United States and France would be permanent members and of which three to five members of the United Nations would be selected in rotation for designated terms by the continental European countries. Voting procedures in the Council for Europe will be settled by the present meeting of the Council of Foreign Ministers.
2. A European Economic and Social Council in which all continental European countries, including the ex-enemy countries and the neutrals, would be represented and which would be provided with a number of subordinate functional organizations or commissions.

The Council for Europe would replace the Deputies of the Foreign Ministers on such unfinished business of the Council of Foreign Ministers as remains in Europe after the conclusion of the present Council meeting and Peace Conference. The Council for Europe would set the terms of reference of the European Economic and Social Council and its subordinate Commissions, reserving to itself or the Security Council of the United Nations the settlement of European problems which affect a security interest in any portion of Europe, and would undertake such other tasks as may be assigned to it by the Security Council of the United Nations.

The European Economic and Social Council would be primarily an administrative and coordinating body for a number of technical commissions, with powers to receive and publish reports of these commissions. It would serve, however, as a formal link between the Commissions and the Economic and Social Council of the United Nations.

Among the possible technical commissions under the European Economic and Social Council, the following are suggested:

(a) Commission on Fuel and Power;
(b) Commission on Inland Transport;
(c) Commission on Telecommunications;
(d) Commission on Trade and Commerce;
(e) Commission on Economic Development;
(f) Commission on Food;
(g) Commission on Finance.

It is proposed that the various Commissions above, and such other commissions as the Council for Europe may deem it desirable to establish, shall include members, who shall be limited to United Nations in or adjacent to Europe; participating observers, including neutral countries (excepting, for the time being, Spain); former enemy countries after the conclusion of treaties; Germany, as represented by the Allied Control Authority; Austria, as represented by the Austrian Government, under such terms as the Allied Council, Austria, may agree; and by observers including the United States, United Kingdom and U.S.S.R., to the extent that those countries are not full members of one or more commissions, such membership being a matter of option. The United States is convinced of the importance of this all-inclusive European participation because it believes that collaboration in the fields of trade, finance, and economic development cannot stop at the borders of neutral countries or ex-enemy states. The representation of the United Kingdom, U.S.S.R. and United States offers no insuperable difficulty. The United States is anxious to give continental Europe maximum opportunity for economic self-determination and is, therefore, willing to confine its participation in the European Economic and Social Council to the role of observer. It realizes, however, that the Soviet Union and United Kingdom have a more direct interest in the economy of continental Europe. It recognizes that these countries may in particular wish to participate fully in the work of those functional organizations of the Council which are of especial concern to them. The Ukraine and Byelo-Russia might be full members of the European Economic and Social Council.

The present meeting of the Council of Foreign Ministers may leave to further negotiation the specific terms of reference of the subordinate commissions with possible ratification by the European members of the Peace Conference called for May 1, and with provision, in any event, for subsequent alteration by the Council for Europe. The United States believes, however, that the terms of reference of the Commissions should be as broad as possible consistent with the ability of the European countries concerned to reach mutually beneficial agreements or recommendations. In any case, the United States proposes that all Commissions be permitted to receive from the member and participating countries such information related to the field of interest of the Commission as such member and participating countries may choose to communicate to it, and to publish such information in a standard form on a regular basis.

With respect to the functions of the specific Commissions listed above, it is proposed that:

(a) *The Commission on Coal and Power be empowered to:*

i) coordinate plans for the revival of coal production in Europe, including the formulation of recommendations concerning the allocation of mining supplies, pit props, etc. available for international exchange, and, in combination with the European Commission on Inland Transport, recommend the allocation of rail and barge capacity involved in the international movement of coal;

ii) recommend allocations of coal imports into European countries on a continent-wide basis, including imports from Ruhr and Silesian mines and imports from overseas, taking into account special agreements regarding coal movements affecting European countries;

iii) foster agreements and understandings for the international transmission of power between or among countries.

(b) *The Commission on Inland Transport be empowered to:*

i) coordinate plans for the revival of European rail, road and inland waterway transport on the basis of freedom of movement on equal terms for all;

ii) exchange information on transport requirements, shortages, accomplishments and recommend to governments concerned improvements in international rail and water transport facilities and schedules;

iii) make arrangements for the maintenance of offices in such countries of Europe, including Germany and Austria, as are essential to the operation of the Commission;

iv) make recommendations regarding the distribution of transport equipment, order of priority of restitution of transport equipment looted from European countries by Germany or by any other ex-enemy country, and the improvement of transit services;

v) make recommendations to member countries on such technical aspects of inland transport as transit charges, rental fees for equipment used in a country not owning such equipment, demurrage, and any other matters that may be agreed as coming within its competence.

(c) *The Commission on Telecommunications be empowered to:*

i) make recommendations on the better distribution of radio frequencies in Europe;

ii) take any practicable steps to bring about improvement in telephone and telegraph communications and allied matters.

(d) *The Commission on Trade and Commerce be empowered to:*

i) during the postwar transition period, make recommendations regarding the most equitable distribution of commodities, other than coal, for importation into European countries.

ii) perform such functions and sponsor such programs and policies, relating to the elimination or reduction of trade barriers, the stimulation of international trade, the promotion of international economic integration, or the raising of European living standards, as are desired by its members and as are not in conflict with the program of the Economic and Social Council, the United Nations, or the proposed International Trade Organization.

iii) encourage the conclusion of modern treaties of friendship, commerce, and establishment by the countries of Europe with each other and with non-European countries, by proposing standard provisions for such treaties and by such other means as may be appropriate.

iv) promote the simplification, standardization, or elimination of legal formalities, documents, and regulations which hamper travel and the free flow of trade within Europe;

v) stimulate the free flow of European technology across national borders by recommending modification of patent legislation, proposing the adoption of uniform principles to govern the dissemination of government-sponsored research and by such other means as may be appropriate with the programs or policies of the Economic and Social Council of the United Nations.

(e) *The Commission on Economic Development be empowered to:*

i) provide a forum for the discussion and reconciliation of the interests of European nations with respect to national reconstruction and development plans;

ii) relate such plans to the allocation of reparations by the IARA in which USSR and Poland may wish to sit as observers;

iii) provide a forum for consultation among the signatories of the Yalta Declaration, in respect to reconstruction of Liberated areas;

iv) draw up plans for European development and for specific development projects involving more than one country; and provide impartial economic and technical assistance to European governments which request such assistance.

(f) *The Commission on Food be empowered to:*

i) cooperate with UNRRA, the Food and Agriculture Organization of the United Nations and similar bodies in collecting information on the production and consumption of food in the various countries of Europe; and in particular on food surpluses and deficits;

ii) recommend the most equitable allocation of overseas foodstuffs available for importation into European countries during the present postwar transition;

iii) recommend to the several countries of Europe changes in agricultural production to those countries during the transition period, designed to make the most effective contribution to the food crisis, and over the longer period to produce a more economic utilization of the land resources of Europe.

(g) *The Commission on Finance be empowered to:*

i) provide a forum in which representatives of central banks and national fiscal authorities discuss and make recommendations on their common problems, including, in particular, the reconstruction of monetary and fiscal systems required as the result of distortions produced by the war period;

ii) develop coordinated programs to combat inflation or deflation and work out common policies on the relationship of fiscal policy to economic development programs.

The United States believes that these proposals will contribute measurably to the pacification and peaceful development of the European continent. The United States has a great stake in the preservation of peace on the European continent in which so many costly wars have begun. It wishes to do everything in its power to provide a guaranteed framework of European collaboration. It eschews imperialism or exclusive sphere of influence. At the same time, it proffers such help as continental Europe may need to work out its destiny free of outside interference. Assuming an organization of Europe in the spirit of these proposals, it stands ready to give such economic assistance as is within its power to all members of the European organization.

APPENDIX B   *SECRET*
CONCRETE PROPOSALS FOR THE SETTLEMENT
OF CERTAIN OUTSTANDING ISSUES

The United States believes that agreement on an organizational framework of European collaboration as outlined in Appendix A would greatly facilitate and should be accompanied by simultaneous settlement of some of the outstanding issues on which the major powers have hitherto failed to agree. These include, in addition to the peace treaties currently under consideration, primarily problems affecting Germany and Austria.

The United States suggests that these outstanding questions might be resolved in the following manner:

1. *Germany*

   An effectively demilitarized and disarmed Germany, deprived of a considerable proportion of its industrial capital equipment under a reparations program, should no longer constitute a menace within the framework of a continental European Organization guaranteed by the Four Major Powers.

   Under these circumstances the United States urges that there be agreement that:

   a) The Saar be incorporated permanently into France.

   b) The Rhineland and Ruhr be retained within Germany.

   c) The Council of Foreign Ministers consider means short of detachment of the Ruhr from Germany, for assuring that its resources be used in common welfare of Europe.

2. *Implementation of Berlin Agreement*

   a) The Allied Control Council be instructed to proceed immediately to the formation of central German administrative agencies, to formulate an import-export program for Germany as a whole, and to expedite the delivery of reparations equipment.

b) The Allied Control Council be instructed to formulate at an early date agreed uniform procedures for the holding of elections throughout Germany.

3. *Austria*

a) The Council of Foreign Ministers undertake immediately to effect a settlement of the question of German assets in Austria.

b) The Allied Council, Austria, be instructed to formulate and put immediately into effect new provisions affecting the control of Austria, which shall include, but not be limited to, the following:

1. Abolition of all zonal restrictions on travel, communication and trade within Austria.
2. The Allied Council, Austria, be instructed to arrange with the Austrian Government the holding of new national elections, sometime shortly after June 1, 1946.
3. The Four Occupying Powers announce their intention to conclude a treaty of final settlement with the Government of Austria by a date not later than January 1, 1947, which will provide for an advisory Commission, representing the Occupying Powers, which will be responsible for the execution of the treaty provisions, and which will report to the Council for Europe.

4. *Danube*

A temporary commission for the Danube be promptly established, based on principles of riparian representation and freedom of navigation, which would be related in a manner symmetrical with other international river commissions to the Economic and Social Council of the United Nations.

Appendix B

Three Press Reports on the Proposal,
April 24–25, 1946

[*Note:* This appendix contains the original Alsop column outlining the Acheson-Clayton proposal and two follow-up news accounts. The source of the initial leak is not known to the author or remembered by Joseph Alsop. At the time it was rumored that Acheson had done the briefing. It was, evidently, accurate and thorough.]

The Washington Post
April 24, 1946

MATTER OF FACT
By Joseph and Stewart Alsop

In Mr. Byrnes' Briefcase

The American delegation to the meeting of the Foreign Ministers has left for Paris in a mood of grim determination not unmixed with despair. They regard it as entirely possible that Soviet intransigeance at the meeting will force the final split of Europe into distinct and irreconcilable eastern and western blocs. In his brief case, however, Secretary of State James F. Byrnes carries a plan to prevent just such a split, if that is possible, by the federation of Europe.

The paper's history is interesting. It was first written in the form of a rough draft by a group of the younger men in the department who felt deeply that some steps must be taken to halt the ever-increasing tendency toward a final division between East and West. The draft moved up through department channels to the desks of Undersecretary Dean Acheson and Assistant Secretary Will Clayton.

Both were enthusiastic, and within the past few weeks presented the plan to the Secretary of State. He was greatly interested and asked for a final revision in detail.

The plan aroused bitter opposition within the department among those who feel that the Russian attitude makes any acceptable settlement impossible. The difficulty lies in obtaining real assurance that the plan will be honestly carried out by the Soviets in the zones of Europe which they control. It is known, however, that Byrnes has taken the final draft of the plan with him to Paris, and he will present it if such assurance is forthcoming.

THE PLAN CALLS for proposing to the Russians an over-all European settlement, whose aim would be to encourage the development of Europe as a political and economic whole. It is thought that it will be easier to solve such specific problems as the Italian peace treaty, the Rhineland-Ruhr proposal, and the various Mediterranean conflicts, if a solution is sought within the framework of a plan for Europe as a whole.

The proposal provides for the extension of the United Nations structure to the formation of a European assembly. This would consist essentially of members of subcommittees, empowered to deal with a range of particular problems on a continent-wide basis. These subcommittees would include all members of the United Nations in Europe, except for England and Russia, and a majority vote would decide any issue. The Security Council would determine the problems with which this European assembly might deal. The great powers, through their membership on the Security Council, would be in a position to veto any decision which might be made by the European assembly.

The range of issues with which the assembly might deal would include fuel and power, trade, transport, finance, planning of capital development, and so on.

The objectors to this plan argue that the decisions of the assembly would not be truly European because of Soviet domination of eastern Europe. But the proponents of this plan do not argue that it would constitute a final solution of the awful problem of the rivalry between Russia and the nations of the west on the Continent. They do argue, however, that it would be a beginning, however modest, toward halting the terrifying European tendency to split for all time into eastern and western blocs.

They argue further that only if it is made clear to all powers that this tendency can be halted, and that the United States is deeply determined that it should be halted, can any reasonable settlement of the grave issues now dividing Russia from the west be expected. For the tendency of the great powers to fly apart into two hostile camps gains appetite by what it feeds on. A division into two mutually suspicious power blocs is already very nearly a fact. Thus the only consideration of importance to any great power is beginning to be the strengthening of its security position on the Continent and elsewhere. Under such circumstances, cooperation for peace will become utterly impossible.

THE PROPOSAL which the Secretary of State carries in his brief case is, and must be, "neutral in terms of security." This means that it does not immediately affect the relative great power relationships which have been established on the Continent since the defeat of Germany. Yet since the plan calls for the encouragement of any independent Europe, functioning more and more as a political whole, and free from domination by any great power, it seems unlikely that it would please the more aggressive of the rulers in the Kremlin. Some of them, at least, certainly look forward to a Europe which would be a political satrapy of the USSR.

Yet in this connection the remarks of Owen Lattimore bear repeating: "The usual discussion of Russia begins and ends with speculation not on what Russia is going to do, but what we are going to do." This plan at least represents a constructive American effort.

In short, the United States, which after all remains the most powerful Nation in the world, must one day cease to act the part of a nervous policeman, and should itself take the initiative. Only thus shall we know whether the world is moving toward peace or toward war, and be able to plan accordingly.

The Washington Post
April 25, 1946

BYRNES TAKES NEW ECONOMIC PLAN TO EUROPE
By John M. Hightower
Associated Press Staff Writer

A new plan to tackle Europe's terrific economic problems on a continent-wide basis, by setting up a United Nations regional office at Geneva, has been taken to Paris by Secretary of State Byrnes.

He may present it to the foreign ministers in a move to break the big-power deadlock over the peace treaties.

This was learned yesterday from persons who are familiar with all details of the proposal but who may not be identified. They said that some of Byrnes' top advisers in the State Department split over the plan and that Byrnes himself has not committed himself to it. But he has indicated keen interest in it as a possible solution to the stalemate confronting him at Paris, where he arrived yesterday.

He had discussed it on several occasions with advisers who favor it, particularly Undersecretary of State Dean Acheson.

The plan is reported to have the support, in some degree at least, of Acheson, State Department Counselor Benjamin V. Cohen, who is with Byrnes in Paris, and Assistant Secretary of State William Clayton. Clayton is in charge of the department's economic affairs and the plan was developed by a group of young economists in his division who are charged with trying to solve German and Austrian economic problems.

Opposition to the proposal stems from the State Department's political division under Assistant Secretary of State James Dunn, who also is with Byrnes in Paris, and particularly the office of European affairs under Freeman Matthews.

Backers of the proposal contend that if Byrnes persists in trying to solve European problems one by one, he will only force a division of Europe into eastern and western spheres in view of Russia's demands.

The new plan calls for a European sub-office of the United Nations beginning with a group representing the Economic and Social Council which would be known as the European Economic Council. Under this would be organized agencies to handle fuel and power, trade and industry, transportation and food. These four would absorb the present European Coal Organization, the Emergency Economic Administration for Europe, the European Central Inland Transport Organization and whatever food machinery now exists.

Eventually, other United Nations machinery for Europe could be set up, possibly including a regional Security Council.

The foreign ministers conference is supposed to write treaties for Italy, the former enemy Balkan states and Finland. It is then supposed to talk about the Ruhr and Rhineland and after that to take up the question of Austria.

That is the pattern which has been followed since last September—without success—and is the one favored for continuance by Byrnes' advisers in the political division of the State Department. As they see it, the Russians either will make arrangements of a compromise kind on major issues or will flatly refuse. In the latter case the last vestige of great power unity in the peace will fall apart into European spheres of influence.

The Acheson-Clayton group contends that at a critical point in the conference Byrnes must have an alternative way of solving the problem. The proposal designed to tackle European peace and reconstruction issues on a continent-wide basis rather than country by country is regarded by them as in line with this principle.

The New York Times
April 25, 1946

BYRNES BEARS EUROPE-WIDE PLAN
FOR GUIDING OF ECONOMY BY U.N.
By Bertram D. Hulen

Washington, April 24—Secretary of State James F. Byrnes was said today to have taken with him to the meeting of the Foreign Ministers in Paris a suggested plan for the solution of European economic problems on a continental basis under the administrative agency of the United Nations. The plan would be for possible use should the conference be unable to make headway in completing separate peace treaties with Italy and other enemy states.

Designed to prevent Europe from breaking into blocs, should the four powers be unable to agree on peace treaties, the plan was prepared by economic specialists in the State Department. It is said to have support to a degree of Dean Acheson, Under-Secretary of State; Benjamin V. Cohen, Counselor of the State Department; and William L. Clayton, Assistant Secretary of State in charge of economic affairs.

However, the plan is opposed by political specialists in the department as unfeasible, and it has not been adopted as yet by Mr. Byrnes as his own. Moreover, it is described as only one of several proposals that the Secretary of State has in his briefcase at Paris for possible use should circumstances lead him to a decision to propose any of them at critical moments in the meeting of the Foreign Ministers.

The economic plan would provide for a European Regional Office of the United Nations at Geneva, probably at first in the form of a commission representing the Economic and Social Council of the United Nations. This would be known as the European Economic Council and would have agencies handling fuel, power, trade, industrial, transportation and food problems. These agencies would absorb the present European Coal Organization, the Emergency Economic Committee for Europe, the European Central Inland Transport Organization, and food machinery.

Supporters of the plan contend that unduly protracted efforts to solve European problems piecemeal, in view of the Russian insistence upon reparations, trusteeships and the like, would bring about a danger of Europe's being permanently divided into Eastern and Western spheres, a result that would be an unstable peace at best.

Opponents of the plan, who are said to include James C. Dunn, Assistant Secretary of State in charge of Geographical Offices in the State Department and Mr. Byrnes' deputy on the Council of Foreign Ministers, and H. Freeman Matthews, chief of the European Office in the State Department—both of whom are with the Secretary of State in Paris—are described as holding that the plan is not workable.

It is admitted by proponents that the feasibility of the plan would turn on the Russian attitude. That is not known.

Appendix C

Telegrams of May 9, 1946,
from Acheson and Hilldring to Byrnes in Paris,
Referring to the Plan

[*Note*: The two following telegrams, from Acheson and Hilldring to Byrnes in Paris, indicate the anxiety of those seeking actively to avoid the split of Germany and Europe, as the Control Council in Berlin moved into crisis over the reparations and central German agencies issue in May 1946. Sections 3, 8, and 9 of the second telegram contain references to the Acheson-Clayton plan "submitted to you prior to your departure."]

SECRET   WASHINGTON, May 9, 1946—7 p.m.
U.S. URGENT

For Secretary from Acheson and Hilldring. Immediately following tel gives background and detailed exposition of plan for your consideration designed as attempt to resolve serious crisis in ACC Germany over relationship of implementation of reparation program to common economic policies and central German agencies. Plan has two features which may be dealt with simultaneously or in any order you consider feasible:

1. Four-Power agreement to negotiate settlement of Ruhr-Rhineland issue, including perhaps related security problems, on ground not only that French acceptance of full-fledged central German agencies hinges on such settlement, but above all that we cannot indefinitely carry out present drastic reparation removals program without definite knowledge whether or not important resources of Ruhr-Rhineland will be available to German economy.

2. Provisional continuation or resumption implementation of reparation program during period of 60–90 days on condition (a) that Soviets agree to join with other powers in immediate in-

structions to ACC to proceed during this period with negotiations on phased plan for adoption and application of common economic policies focussed on adoption of export-import program based on certain pre-agreed principles outlined in subsequent tel and with understanding implementation common policies would be entrusted, pending establishment full-fledged German central agencies, to quadripartite allied bureaus assisted by staffs of German technical experts, and (b) that further implementation of reparation would be immediately suspended if no substantial progress made in this period in negotiations on treatment of Germany as economic unit.

Whole plan is designed to avoid threatened breakup of ACC, to remove principal blocks to reparation program, and above all, to put Soviet protestations of loyalty to Potsdam to final test in order to gauge their willingness to live up to substance as well as letter of Potsdam and fix blame for breach of Potsdam on Soviets in case they fail to meet this test.

Sent to Paris, repeated to USPolAd, Berlin as Dept's 1074.

[Acheson and Hilldring.]

ACHESON

SECRET   WASHINGTON, May 9, 1946—7 p.m.
U.S. URGENT

Secdel 219. Following is background and more detailed exposition of proposals in immediately preceding tel to Sec. State from Acheson and Hilldring.

1. We fully endorse Clay's stand on essential interrelationship of reparation plan and treatment of Germany as economic unit. Unless Russians give convincing demonstration they are prepared to adopt and implement common economic policies now, there is no assurance that Germany will be treated as economic unit after 2-year period of reparation removals and that accordingly amount of capital equipment left to Germany will suffice to enable Germany or separate parts of Germany to live on average continental European standard of living without outside assistance, as Potsdam requires. Similarly, early decision on Ruhr-Rhineland issue appears necessary not only to remove French opposition to German central agencies, but above all to enable General Clay to take initiative for drastic revision, if not total abandonment of present reparation plan, in

event resources of Ruhr-Rhineland unavailable to German economy. Therefore desirable in our opinion to induce Russians to discuss both Ruhr-Rhineland and program for real implementation of Potsdam provision for treatment of Germany as unit.

2. Current Soviet policy believed to be motivated by one or more of following considerations:

a) Conviction that split of Europe into Eastern and Western oriented blocs is inevitable or desirable and that accordingly it must keep Eastern Germany as well as all of Eastern and Southeastern Europe firmly under Soviet unilateral control;

b) Necessity of retaining or consolidating firm Soviet economic and political control of Soviet zone until time when unification of Germany can take place under conditions most advantageous to Soviets;

c) Fear that application of common economic policies to Germany as a whole would interfere with present Soviet practices of obtaining reparation from own zone, including reparation from current output, without reference to economic plan for all of Germany, and would impose on Soviets, who now have most self-sufficient zone, burden of meeting part of deficits of other less self-sufficient zones.

3. In this connection it is our understanding that US insistence on treatment of Germany as economic unit has been motivated primarily by US interest in preventing permanent division of Germany into two antagonistic halves corresponding to our interest in preventing split of Europe as whole into irreconcilable blocs and definitive failure of four-power collaboration. This objective fits in with your proposal for four-power 25-year treaty of guaranty and proposal, discussed with you prior to your departure, to establish organized framework for economic collaboration of all continental European countries on basis of equality.

4. Desire to reduce cost of occupation by reducing over-all German trade deficit through pooling of German economic resources and by providing for equitable sharing among all occupying powers of burden of financing this deficit until Germany can be made self-sustaining also motivates US insistence on treatment of Germany as economic unit, but is of secondary importance. We fully agree that cost of occupation of all four powers together would be reduced by adoption of common policies and export-import program for Ger-

many as a whole. However, if Soviet reluctant to share in any substantial measure deficit of other zones, it might be worthwhile in order to achieve treatment of Germany as economic unit for US to suggest that the cost of financing any net import deficit under agreed export-import program might be shared proportionately by occupying powers in such manner as not to impose any substantial increase in relative burden of Soviets.

5. Basic problem is for US Govt to devise a practicable plan which would provide strong support for Clay's stand on integral execution of Potsdam. In our opinion such plan should be designed to force Soviet Union to show its real attitude toward unification of Germany within European framework and to avoid any danger that Soviets might put onus of breaking with Potsdam on US. In this connection it must be borne in mind that while Soviets first insisted in Economic Directorate meeting of April 5 on continued handling of German foreign trade on zonal basis until reparation plan was carried out in full and/or it became possible to achieve a trade balance for Germany as whole, all of which was complete negation of Potsdam, they later retreated from this extreme position and sought to reconcile their position at least with letter of Potsdam. In Economic Directorate meeting April 18, for example, Soviets agreed that Germany should be treated as economic unit and that steps should be taken to devise export-import program for Germany as whole, with proviso that in such program "account shall be taken, where appropriate, of local conditions" according to phraseology of para 14, Section III [11] of Potsdam Protocol and that therefore in immediate future trade should be conducted on zonal basis within net balance of each zone. This stand reiterated by Soviets in Coordinating Committee meeting of April 26. In Coordinating Committee meeting May 3, Russians went on record as endorsing common import-export program but sought delay in discussions until process of selecting all plants surplus to capacity left to Germany under Level of Industry Agreement and therefore available for reparation was completed and decision was reached on plants to be destroyed as war potential. While these shifting Russian tactics cast serious doubt on Russian willingness to put into effect Potsdam provisions on treatment Germany as economic unit, it is clear that Russians are cleverly seeking to reconcile their position with letter of Potsdam in order to put onus for breaking with

Potsdam on other powers. For this reason, we consider it important to confront Russians with a plan which will really put their protestations of loyalty to Potsdam to a test and place onus for failure of Potsdam on them in event they do not meet the test.

6. Essence of such a plan in our opinion would be simultaneous implementation of reparation plan and development and application of program for common policies. In view of failure of Potsdam to stipulate schedule for implementation its provisions, it is difficult to argue that common policies should precede reparation or vice versa. In essence they should march hand in hand. Neither can be accomplished overnight. Indefinite suspension of reparation program may well involve break up of ACC, although it might be possible for brief period to avoid definitive break by continuing, as Clay proposes, paper allocation of plants for reparation and holding up actual deliveries. It may also be mentioned that suspension of reparation would adversely affect reparation claimants other than Soviets and that provisional continuation of reparation deliveries in immediate future would not unduly prejudice our position in view of fact that reparation removals would in any event owing to their volume be spaced over two full years. Suspension of reparation deliveries might also force British into unilateral removals from their zone—action which they have already threatened to take once before in view of delay in carrying out reparation program.

7. In light of above, we present for your consideration and consultation with Clay and Murphy, a plan which, while based on full endorsement of Clay's position on interrelationship of reparation plan and treatment of Germany as economic unit, would provide for continued or resumed implementation of reparation program during a period of 60–90 days on condition that Soviets agree to join with other occupying powers in instructions to ACC to proceed during this period with negotiations on a phased plan for the adoption and implementation of common economic policies focussed on adoption of export-import program which shall be based on:—

a) pooling of German economic resources through free interzonal trade, thereby reducing import needs for Germany as a whole;

b) allocation of imported and indigenous materials in such a manner as to attain uniform rate of economic recovery in all zones and allocation of German production as between domestic consumption and exports in such a way as to maintain some fixed differential in rate of German economic recovery and that of rest of continental Europe;

c) explicit understanding that exports from current output and stocks will be used only to pay imports into Germany until all past imports are paid for and Germany can be made self-sustaining. (It must be recognized that Potsdam Protocol does not explicitly rule out reparation from current output as far as Soviet zone is concerned and that this ambiguity should be cleared up.)

d) understanding, if required to obtain Soviet support, that the burden of financing any temporary surplus of imports over exports will be shared by the occupying powers in manner indicated in para 4 above.

Negotiations on common policies should in our opinion also be based on understanding that implementation of such policies should, pending establishment of central German administrative departments, be entrusted to quadripartite allied agencies such as proposed Export-Import Bureau which would be assisted by staff of German technical experts. It is our understanding French would agree to such a proposal. In this connection it might be pointed out that France as nonsignatory of Potsdam Protocol, is under no obligation to assent to central German agencies and that central German agencies would in any event be unable to operate successfully without agreed quadripartite control and direction.

Scope of negotiations on common policies might also include efforts to obtain common policies in certain fields in which Soviets profess to have an interest similar to US such as effective action against German combines and trusts called for in para 12, Section III [11] of Potsdam Protocol and efforts to secure agreement on division of large estates and on nationalization of properties of combines, convicted Nazis and war criminals, etc., in order to eliminate classes which supported Nazism and extreme German nationalism in past. By taking initiative in these questions we would avoid the charge that we were seeking to impose a "Western capitalist" orientation on Germany and we would, through vigorous championing of economic and social reforms which would lay basis for economic as well as political democracy. We can certainly also afford to meet the Russian challenge regarding complete disarmament of Germany, particularly total prohibition of manufacture of all armament. While there is evidence that all occupying powers still tolerate manufacture of armament in their zones to varying degrees, the Soviets have apparently been the principal offenders by re-equipping aviation squadrons with jet aircraft and fleet with "schnorkel" submarines produced in Soviet zone; French are also producing some armament; and even US is engaged in some manufacture for experimental purposes in its zone. These facts particularly relevant to reported Molotov reaction to your proposal for 25-year treaty of guaranty and you may accordingly find it advisable to propose inspection of disarmament progress all zones.

Continuation of reparation program during this test period would be subject to explicit understanding that (1) additional removals from Soviet zone shall take into account necessity of capital equipment for Germany as a whole within agreed Level of Industry Plan (In this connection it should be pointed out Soviets are removing sugar beet processing factories from Tangermuende area on Elbe even though plants are not surplus to German requirements as whole and Level of Industry Agreement makes no provision for removal of such plants from Germany), and (2) immediate steps will be taken to activate mixed commissions for task of assessing present industrial capacity in all zones and to apportion among four zones capacity left to Germany under Level of Industry Agreement. Essential part of plan would be immediate suspension further implementation of reparation plan at end of test period if no substantial progress made in negotiations on treatment of Germany as economic unit.

8. Above plan in our judgment has merit of being based squarely on Potsdam, of avoiding any imputation that US is abandoning Potsdam, and of forcing Soviets to reveal whether in fact they will live up to substance as well as letter of Potsdam. Consensus here that if you judge plan feasible, it might be advisable for the sake of bargaining, to broach it to Soviets in way which would indicate to them clearly that, while US is firmly convinced of desirability of treating Germany as an economic unit within framework of European economic system, it would have to consider, in event of failure of other powers to agree on effective implementation of this policy, disagreeable but inevitable alternative of treating Western Germany as economic unit and integrating this unit closely with Western European economy. You may wish to emphasize that US would greatly

prefer to maintain Germany as unit under effective quadripartite control and to fit Germany as unit into a framework of organized continental European economic collaboration as proposed in the plan submitted to you prior to your departure, but that unwillingness of Soviets to cooperate would leave US with no choice other than alternative plan.

9. It is suggested that it might also be desirable to link negotiations on common policies under plan outlined above with simultaneous negotiations on Ruhr-Rhineland. Since, as we understand, Soviets have so far refused to have Ruhr-Rhineland placed on conference agenda, it might be pointed out to them that we cannot indefinitely continue implementation of reparation plan without an early decision on fate of Ruhr-Rhineland. You will recall that both War Dept and Gen Clay have strongly urged necessity of prompt resolution of this issue. Another objective of negotiations would be to remove French opposition to establishment central Germany agencies. Negotiations on Ruhr-Rhineland might be broadened to include whole security issue, including your proposal for 25-year treaty of guaranty and, if you deem wise, plan for European economic collaboration. While it may be impossible to obtain immediate consideration Ruhr-Rhineland issue, we feel that indefinite postponement would be incompatible in the end with continued execution of reparation plan.

Sent to Paris, repeated to USPolAd Berlin as Dept's 1075.

ACHESON

Appendix D

George Kennan's "Practical Deductions"
from the Analysis in His "Long Cable"
of February 1946

[*Note*: This appendix contains the final portion of George Kennan's "long cable" of February 1946, with its broad "practical deductions" for U.S. policy. The emphasis on the importance of the U.S. domestic performance to U.S.-Soviet relations remains at least as relevant to the 1980s as to the immediate postwar years. As noted in the text, Kennan did not include in this cable his strongly held view (as of 1945 and 1946) that the split of Europe should be accepted and a Western bloc built.]

Practical Deductions from Standpoint of US Policy.

In summary, we have here a political force committed fanatically to the belief that with US there can be no permanent modus vivendi, that it is desirable and necessary that the internal harmony of our society be disrupted, our traditional way of life be destroyed, the international authority of our state be broken, if Soviet power is to be secure. This political force has complete power of disposition over energies of one of the world's greatest peoples and resources of the world's richest national territory, and is borne along by deep and powerful currents of Russian nationalism. In addition, it has an elaborate and far-flung apparatus for exertion of its influence in other countries, an apparatus of amazing flexibility and versatility, managed by people whose experience and skill in underground methods are presumably without parallel in history. Finally, it is seemingly inaccessible to considerations of reality in its basic reactions. For it, the vast fund of objective fact about human society is not, as with us, the measure against which outlook is constantly being tested and reformed, but a grab bag from which individual items are selected arbitrarily and tendentiously to bolster an outlook already preconceived. This is admittedly not a pleasant picture. Problem of how to cope with this force is undoubtedly greatest task our diplomacy has ever faced and probably the greatest it will ever have to face. It should be the point of departure from which our political general staff work at the present juncture should proceed. It should be approached with same thoroughness and care as solution of major strategic problem in war, and if necessary, with no smaller outlay in planning effort. I cannot attempt to suggest all the answers here. But I would like to record my conviction that the problem is within our power to solve—and that without recourse to any general military conflict. And in support of this conviction there are certain observations of a more encouraging nature I should like to make.

(One) Soviet power, unlike that of Hitlerite Germany, is neither schematic nor adventuristic. It does not work by fixed plans. It does not take unnecessary risks. Impervious to logic of reason, and it is highly sensitive to logic of force. For this reason it can easily withdraw—and usually does—when strong resistance is encountered at any point. Thus, if the adversary has sufficient force and makes clear his readiness to use it, he rarely has to do so. If situations are properly handled there need be no prestige-engaging showdowns.

(Two) Gauged against Western world as a whole, Soviets are still by far the weaker force. Thus, their success will really depend on degree of cohesion, firmness, and vigor which Western world can muster. And this is factor which it is within our power to influence.

(Three) Success of Soviet system, as form of internal power, is not yet finally proven. It has yet to be demonstrated that it can survive supreme test of successive transfer of power from one individual or group to another. Lenin's death was first such transfer, and its effects wracked Soviet state for fifteen years after. Stalin's death or retirement will be second. But even this will not be final test. Soviet internal system will now be subjected, by virtue of recent territorial expansions, to a series of additional strains which once proved severe tax on Tsardom. We here are convinced that never since termination of the civil war have the mass of Russian people been emotionally farther removed from doctrines of Communist Party than they are today. In Russia, party has now become a great and—for the moment—highly successful apparatus of dictatorial administration, but it has ceased to be a source of emotional inspiration. Thus, internal soundness and permanence of movement need not yet be regarded as assured.

(Four) All Soviet propaganda beyond Soviet security sphere is basically negative and destructive. It should therefore be relatively easy to combat it by any intelligent and really constructive program.

For these reasons I think we may approach calmly and with good heart the problem of how to deal with Russia. As to how this approach should be made, I only wish to advance, by way of conclusion, the following comments:

1. Our first step must be to apprehend, and recognize for what it is, the nature of the movement with which we are dealing. We must study it with the same courage, detachment, objectivity, and the same determination not to be emotionally provoked or unseated by it, with which a doctor studies unruly and unreasonable individuals.

2. We must see that our public is educated to realities of Russian situation. I cannot overemphasize the importance of this. Press cannot do this alone. It must be done mainly by government, which is necessarily more experienced and better informed on practical problems involved. In this we need not be deterred by ugliness of the picture. I am convinced that there would be far less hysterical anti-Sovietism in our country today if the realities of this situation were better understood by our people. There is nothing as dangerous or as terrifying as the unknown. It may also be argued that to reveal more information on our difficulties with Russia would reflect unfavorably on Russian-American relations. I feel that if there is any real risk here involved, it is one which we should have the courage to face, and the sooner the better. But I cannot see what we would be risking. Our stake in this country, even coming on the heels of tremendous demonstrations of our friendship for Russian people, is remarkably small. We have here no investments to guard, no actual trade to lose, virtually no citizens to protect, few cultural contacts to preserve. Our only stake lies in what we hope rather than what we have; and I am convinced we have a better chance of realizing those hopes if our public is enlightened and if our dealings with Russians are placed entirely on realistic and matter of fact basis.

3. Much depends on health and vigor of our own society. World communism is like malignant parasite which feeds only on diseased

tissue. This is the point at which domestic and foreign policies meet. Every courageous and incisive measure to solve internal problems of our own society, to improve self-confidence, discipline, morale, and community spirit of our own people, is a diplomatic victory over Moscow worth a thousand diplomatic notes and joint communiqués. If we cannot abandon fatalism and indifference in face of deficiencies of our own society, Moscow will profit— Moscow cannot help profiting by them in its foreign policies.

4. We must formulate and put forward for other nations a much more positive and constructive picture of the sort of world we would like to see than we have put forward in the past. It is not enough to urge the people to develop political processes similar to our own. Many foreign peoples, in Europe at least, are tired and frightened by experiences of the past, and are less interested in abstract freedom than in security. They are seeking guidance rather than responsibilities. We should be better able than the Russians to give them this. And unless we do, the Russians certainly will.

5. Finally, we must have courage and self-confidence to cling to our own methods and conceptions of human society. After all, the greatest danger that can befall us in coping with this problem of Soviet communism is that we shall allow ourselves to become like those with whom we are coping.

Appendix E

Rostow to Kindleberger Memorandum of June 10, 1946, Reporting on His Trip to Berlin and Paris

[*Note*: This memorandum to Kindleberger from me of June 10, 1946, reports on matters not covered by cables sent to Washington while in Berlin. The mission on which I was sent (with J. K. Galbraith) concerned the desire in Washington to induce Clay to join the State Department in inducing the British to provide at higher priority the resources (including food for the miners) to permit Ruhr coal production to expand. Aside from telling the reader more than he wishes to know about the coal issue in June 1946, the memorandum does capture the still hopeful mood about U.S.-Soviet relations in the Control Council, despite the May 1946 breakdown on reparations, impressions of Berlin itself and German thought about European unity, the mood in Paris about the treaty negotiations, and other assorted gossip which may evoke something of Europe in mid 1946.]

C.P. Kindleberger   JUNE 10, 1946
W.W. Rostow
Coal and Other Matters

1. Following are informal reflections on the problem of coal production and other matters encountered on my recent trip. I group these roughly under: Coal, USSR relations, France, the British, Miscellaneous.

COAL

2. The analysis of the operation of the British Zone and its coal mines which emerged from conversations in Berlin is not hopeful. The recommendations we made, and agreed with OMGUS [Office of Military Government, U.S.], are palliatives; and more thoroughgoing action will be, in fact, required if an increase in production is to be

sustained. It is doubted by many in Berlin whether the British now in Germany are likely or capable of carrying out the requisite action.

3. The organization of economic activity in the British Zone has left power over resources distributed at various levels, and has minimized the influence of central planning. Some 3000 economic officers operate and build their empires down to Kreis level; and there has been inadequate co-ordination and planning among the coal, transport, steel, and other higher level elements. It is significant that the coal people at Essen were neither consulted nor informed before the de-nazification purge of mine technicians; and, incidentally, even Robertson was not informed before the ration cut in the British Zone. Brig. Marley, British coal chief, is judged a weak man by our people; and Sir Percy Mills, who is regarded in quadripartite negotiations as a strong figure, is believed to have very dilute power over the economic operations in the British Zone.

4. The new economic plan for the third quarter on which the British are now working—successor to the ill-fated and ill-named Spartan Plan—represents an attempt at over-all planning in the zone. It seems unlikely to be effective unless accompanied by a tightening and centralization of administrative power.

5. The new economic plan calls for coal consumption in the zone—presumably exclusive of pit-head consumption—of about 8 million tons for the quarter; steel production of 900,000 tons; steel allocation to the mines of 150,000 tons.

6. In addition to the increased steel allocation to the mines, the British have shown the following responses to the pressure the French and US Governments have exerted:

   a) British and German four-man coal efficiency teams are now touring the British Zone and will report in about two weeks on coal wastage and means for its elimination;

   b) British officials privately admit the cut in miners' rations was a mistake;

   c) Shinwell has recently visited Essen.

7. Herr Bauer, Chief German coal man from the American Zone, wrote a report on a recent visit to the Ruhr for OMGUS. He emphasized the food problem; the need for backing and responsibility for mine managers without fear of further de-nazification; the need for some increase in the Reichsmark price of coal, and an end to the

open-end loans the British are making to the mines. He said that he was struck by the extremely low level of discipline in the mines.

8. In mine administration Clay and his staff agree that the British have fallen between two stools: they have not supplied sufficient British staff to operate the mines; but they intrude on working levels in a manner such as to justify and even encourage the Germans to evade responsibility. It is Clay's firm conviction that they should withdraw to a level of policy making, surveillance, planning, and inspection, leaving clearly defined responsibility and authority at medium and lower levels. It is basically the confusion of British administration at the present time which has made OMGUS sceptical of the efficacy of further advisers, technicians, etc.

9. Under Bauer's leadership the US Zone German officials are considering the offer of some potatoes, fish, tobacco, and heavy clothing to the Ruhr miners.

10. On the Reichsmark coal price the British have proposed an increase of from 15 to 25 Reichsmarks per ton. Bauer obtained from old friends sample cost analyses and told [William] Draper that in his judgment an average increase of 10 Reichsmarks or less could only be justified at this time. US Zone officials think that a subsidy would be preferable to a price increase.

11. Bauer stated as the opinion of Ruhr operators that there was no need to worry about the size of the labor force in the mines: in the short run the problem is productivity and in the long run the labor force can be recruited, if adequate incentives are offered. It appears to be a fact, however, that the working force at the present time includes a good many very young men and boys and a great many old members of the working force, with the intervening age classes poorly represented. Incidentally, Bauer urged that the PW [prisoner of war] miners in Belgium and France be returned to Germany. When it was pointed out that they are fed better and are more productive abroad he remarked to Draper: "How many calories for homesickness"?

12. In conversation about coal the British in Berlin made the following points, in a generally defensive manner:

    a) the "responsibility" of owning the Ruhr precludes leaving a larger share of management in German hands;

    b) the failure to allocate larger quantities of steel to the mines in the past was due to the priority of other requirements for steel;

c) the extraordinary pit-head consumption of coal—more than 19% of total production—is due to the fact that the overheads are constant for power and so forth at any level of production;

d) "too much coal" was exported in the second half of 1945.

Galbraith and I did not take the occasion of arguing these points, feeling that the job of needling rested with OMGUS. We asked certain questions.

13. Pete Martin explained to us that the OMGUS attitude towards this problem was for long colored by the feeling that, despite the inadequacies of the British, their claim to large coal consumption was in the American interest, since recovery in the US Zone would be, largely, a function of that in the UK Zone. In recent weeks they have come to accept the likelihood that, without a more serious priority approach to coal mining, revival in production might be indefinitely delayed; and OMGUS as a whole was rather more than we could surmise in a mood to press the British hard on specific measures to increase coal production.

14. With respect to allocations for domestic consumption versus exports, Draper proposed that any increases over the present level be split proportionally as between the two channels: tending to perpetuate the present 75% – 25% split. We suggested that this might prove unfair to the countries dependent on German exports. He recognized this possibility; but envisaged that such a formula would be for a short-period only, covering in all probability a small over-all increase in production. We reserved the Department's position. In the meanwhile, Brig. Anderson, Percy Mills' man on coal, is working on a more elaborate formula, suggested by Ripman's signal to Berlin, after talking with GA. It involves progressive increases in the percentage exported, as production increases, starting with the present level, and present split, and moving towards the calculated level of industry domestic consumption and export. He has made his rough initial calculations for the three western zones, making the assumptions:

a) that USSR Zone would be self-sufficient;

b) that the level of industry consumption in the USSR Zone

would be at the rate of 29 million tons hard coal equivalent a year, a figure given by the Soviets in a working committee.

This implied, ultimately, 81 million tons consumption in the three western zones, and 45 million tons exports. The general shape of Anderson's curves showed a more rapid increase in German domestic consumption in the early stages; and rapid rise in exports in the latter stages:—a pattern on which the French will undoubtedly take the occasion to comment.

15. In general, the US and UK Zones seem near to the point in coal consumption where small increases in consumption will produce large increases in industrial production; over the early stages, of course, the bulk of consumption falls in public utilities, transport, and other over-head items. Clay and Draper remarked that with an extra 200,000 tons per month they could reactivate a very substantial industry in the US Zone. This is, on the whole, a hopeful factor; and it also accounts in part for the tantalized attitude of OMGUS officials with respect to coal production and exports.

USSR RELATIONS

16. As we have already gathered the OMGUS attitude towards the Soviets is one of cautious optimism. They feel, out of their experience, that hard-bargaining straight-forward Americans who know their objectives, and who have reasonable objectives, can do business with the Russians. They emphasize the need for clarity, simplicity, and directness in all relations; and out of the experience in Berlin a series of firm personal relations have grown up. At the top this attitude of mind is universal, at lower levels probably somewhat more spotty. The sense of mission felt at the top is signified by Draper's remark that should the Control Council fold tomorrow, he would still regard its operations as having made an important contribution to our long-run relations with the USSR.

17. Koval's assistant (K. is Draper's opposite number) has remarked that real treatment of Germany as an economic unit can not take place until the Army commanders are eliminated from Germany or their economic powers seriously reduced. Economic policy in the Soviet Zone is, apparently, made up of at least three elements: general planning in Berlin; reparations, operated independently and with over-riding priority, from Moscow; and the regional operations of the military commanders. Soviet Zone stories of confused direction and divided authority had a familiar ring.

18. It is the conviction in Berlin that Soviet policy has up to the present consistently looked towards treating Germany as an economic unit. Recent events have not altered that general view; although it is evident that the Soviets are in less of a hurry than the US. The following evidences, from current events, were cited of USSR intentions in this respect:

a) a new and announced "final" wave of removals;
b) Soviet encouragement of relations between German businessmen and officials, in the various zones;
c) continued and explicit assertion of loyalty, in ACA committees, to the Potsdam "economic unit" provisions;
d) conciliatory approaches to Murphy from his Soviet opposite number.

Whether correct or not it is the Berlin view that Clay's hold-up of reparations is designed rather more to get the French obstruction cleared up than to show up Soviet intentions; there is no question, however, that at the very least it is forcing the pace on the Soviets.

19. I spent an evening's conversation with the German who is charged, under Koval, with economic operations in the Soviet Zone. He says—and Don Heath strongly confirms—that he is not a Communist. He spent 1942–45 in Sachsenhausen (Oranienburg), a political concentration camp for Germans and western Europeans. He was a small businessman in the electrical engineering trade, who was vaguely associated by the Nazis with persons who were engaged in an anti-Hitler plot, who were executed in 1942. He regards the Control Council operation and his own and other "good" Germans' activities as two parts of the same process of finding a way for the East and West to live together. He believes that a German position as a "bridge" rather than a bargaining weapon between East and West can only be achieved through a united Europe, a conception he and his colleagues at Sachsenhausen explored at length during the war (several are now in Cabinet positions in various European governments, and they still correspond regularly). He says that the Soviets are undergoing a great historical process, in becoming involved intimately with the west; that they are being deeply influenced by such various forces as General Clay and German women; and that we must not lose patience. It will take time, but there are hopeful signs. He said the Russians are honestly very suspicious of US motives. He himself has shared with

the Berlin Russians the vagaries of split Soviet economic policy, including especially the ubiquitous and powerful reparations boys who turn up at odd places, disrupting plans. He fought through in a recent legal battle (I believe in Saxony) an interesting point: the Soviets wished to take into government ownership a very wide range of industrial properties, without compensation. He and other Germans succeeded in getting the list much reduced, and in getting compensation agreed for all but war criminals. I can not judge the extent or substance of this alleged victory. He gave the impression of a canny man, not without strength and a certain idealism, for things larger than German nationalism. Incidentally, while we were in Germany, the Heidelberg students came out for a United States of Europe.

20. As a quadripartite town Berlin is a mighty strange place. The Russian soldiers still have a bad reputation; and the Germans in their zone do not wear their best clothes. The ruins are monumental to the point of grandeur. The streets are clear. Bricks are being slowly cleaned and stacked. There is a remarkably good theatrical, concert, and opera season on; and I am told that very intense political discussion takes place, and a vigorous political life exists among the group of Germans concerned. Colonel Busby, US Provost-Marshal with whom we flew in, says the US Zone, Berlin, blotter is almost identical on a per capita basis with that of Los Angeles, quantitatively; although the constitution of crime differs somewhat. A good many people look thin; and a good many OK, but starving folk don't appear on the streets, and I had no shoe-shine conversations.

FRANCE

21. The French—or rather France—is in very bad odor with the US element in Berlin. They feel that the US Government gave them a job to negotiate out with the Soviets, and then tied their hands by leaving the terms of the deal open-end with respect to the French. Galbraith and I took an hour or so at dinner one night playing devil's advocate for the French; but found, as might have been predicted, that one can only succeed by agreeing that the Department has let them down to the extent that we failed to force an early and definitive resolution of the Rhineland-Ruhr issue. Personally it is believed at OMGUS that the French in Berlin are out of

sympathy with their instructions; and have a more lively sense of the significance of the effort at quadripartite government.

22. The meetings of the [Foreign Ministers] Deputies in Paris are disheartening. Everyone works very hard, late into each night; but they are aiming merely at a definition of differences. As compared with Berlin two things were striking:

a) the Council of Foreign Ministers lacks the progressive stages of staff work, leading to the top, by which differences of view may be ironed out;

b) there is a much lesser tendency to "lean in", and seek the compromise solution.

I attended a discussion of the Italian treaty economic provisions. It was clear that, at the working level, a great many points of difference, many small, would emerge from the negotiation. To pass such detailed and technical matters directly to the top, for compromise or other resolution, without one or more intermediate stages of negotiation by higher authority, with power and will to compromise, appeared, especially after Berlin, to be a hopeless procedure.

23. I do not pretend to be expert in French politics. It is evident, however, that the central problem will remain to give adequate effect to the democratic shift to the Right, while still holding the Communists whole-heartedly in the Government. The power over the economy held by the Communists, with its positive aspect rooted in the successful coal production drive, its negative aspect in the threat of large and inflationary wage increases, or in strikes, is decisive; and unlikely to be broken. The implication of this fact for a western bloc, and its stability, is obvious; and it seems clear that if France is to proceed peacefully towards recovery and reconstruction, the delicate process of negotiation among the parties must continue; and this relationship, undoubtedly shared in many other governments in Europe, should prove a very strong force for One Europe, rather than Two.

24. Paris, after Berlin, is heartening. From haystacks all over France cars have emerged, and are driven uniformly at 90 miles an hour. About three a day wrap themselves around trees along the Champs Elysées. The food situation is still bad at the periphery of working-class folk, without access to country-side or black market; but not the central problem it was. The harvests look good. I attended a

technical exhibit in Paris, with Mr. Dunn and party, devoted to machines, furniture, ice-boxes, etc. Mostly prototype stuff, I assume. The furniture was in such bad and heavy taste that for the first time I was concerned by the possible long-run effect of German Occupation; but I assume that better will come. There are many newly published books available; and the shops have things in them, although thinner than they look.

25. Mr. Little, of the US Embassy, Paris, commented on the return, with recovery, of two familiar national characteristics: the venality of the small bureaucrat (and perhaps the large); the strong adherence to investment in gold and hard currency, which will undoubtedly be a factor with which the Monnet Plan will have to contend.

THE BRITISH

26. Americans engaged in quadripartite negotiations in both Berlin and in Paris expressed identical dissatisfaction with their British colleagues; namely, that in relations with the Russians, they tend to be, on the whole, pompous, stiff, and often unnecessarily nasty: "trying to put the Russians in their place", as it was described. Aside from large policy matters it is my own guess—as an old Britisher—that this results partly from enforced contact with persons whose manners often indicate that they haven't been to a good school; or more seriously, the Soviet approach to working level negotiations is apparently direct, vigorous, and challenging in a manner that Americans find easier to deal with than Britishers. It could be written off as an unimportant fact of international life but for the fact that the whole process of quadripartite negotiation seems seriously affected by it. Several OMGUS personnel engaged in such negotiations remarked that the Soviet element tends to break off and retire to its discussion tents after what our people regard as pettish and totally fruitless British outbreaks. This may prove, over a period of time, a real problem for our people, since the British back our lead consistently; so consistently, that our people tend to find occasion to take public issue with them. In Berlin this feeling is exacerbated by the judgment that the British are only supporting the quadripartite experiment verbally. They will follow our lead; but they have made little constructive contribution. A notable exception to this observation appears to be Sir Percy Mills, Draper's opposite number, a

strong out-spoken man, who has everyone's respect. He leaves shortly, to Draper's regret. [Jacques] Reinstein's British opposite number in Paris, on the other hand, is an over-worked, worried, small civil servant type, who is frightened of and hates the large, tough, able Russian who sits on the sub-committee. The Britisher takes it out in as bitter light verse as I've ever seen. Our people respect the Russian, who has the rare quality for a Soviet negotiator of being intellectually responsive; that is, he attempts to meet head-on the arguments supporting our position, and to buttress fully in exposition the position given him from Moscow. He is, however, given to occasional speeches, which our folk resent about equally with the Britisher's statements beginning: "It is the view of His Majesty's Government. . . ." The French, on issues other than high national French policy, try to be helpful and compromising, in both Berlin and Paris.

27. I return convinced, along with US people in Berlin and London (ECO), that the British are doing a very bad job in the Ruhr, for a complex of reasons that I can not pretend accurately to weight; and that no good purpose is likely to be served by not making this judgment clear to them. Better, we should settle as soon as possible—and make operational whatever international controls are agreed should persist.

28. Conversations with various Britishers in London leave the impression that the Labor Government is doing reasonably well; and that some of the younger men in the Party are making some headway. [John] Strachey's supplanting of Ben Smith is, of course, the clearest case of this. It seems, at the moment, a distinctly stable government; although the Beaverbrook press is carrying out one of the most rabid campaigns I've ever seen, even in US. It made hay of the Department's disclaimer on Morrison's food statement.

29. Geoffrey Crowther at dinner took the position that he didn't know, in the present crisis in Germany, whether he wanted One world or Two for Europe, saying that it might be a good idea if the Russians "stewed in their juice" in Eastern Europe. He assumed, at first implicitly, full US support for a Western bloc. In general, in this and other conversations in London, I found the British, less than the French but still strikingly, focussed on limited, rather old national interests:—a kind of provincialism. It is of course understandable;

but it underlined the rather special attitude of the Americans in Berlin who are focussed on a large goal, not superficially related to a direct American interest, in the usual sense.

MISCELLANEOUS

30. There is operating in Europe an allegedly American air line called MATS. It almost killed Covey Oliver. It has no technicians for servicing; no regular schedules; and no apparent means of communication between air fields. Planes leave when they leave, arrive when they arrive. People wait four hours and are blandly told Flight 419, as it is named *ex tempore*, will not fly today. It is strictly a Balkan or Banana Republic operation, to be avoided if at all possible and is clearly subversive.

31. I flew home in a Constellation. It is a hot ship—the Marauder among the transports: high wing loading, long take-off and landing runs; subject to small engine difficulties; and so sensitive in the air that it requires almost continuous manual flying. Cruises at 230 mph air speed with engines throttled back to 900 hp. But they serve cocktails before dinner!

GA:WWRostow:shp   6/11/46

Appendix F

Churchill's Zurich Speech of September 19, 1946, in Support of European Unity

[*Note*: The text of Churchill's famous Zurich speech of September 19, 1946, in support of European unity is of interest as the first such pronouncement by a major statesman after the Second World War; for its emphasis on the initial role of French-German reconciliation, implicitly leaving Britain out of a unified Europe; and for its hedge, toward the end, on how far east a unified Europe might run.]

A UNITED STATES OF EUROPE
FRANCE AND GERMANY MUST LEAD THE WAY
By WINSTON CHURCHILL, Former Prime Minister of Great Britain
Delivered at Zurich University, Zurich, Switzerland,
September 19, 1946

I am honored today by being received in your ancient university and by the address which has been given to me on your behalf and which I greatly value. I wish to speak to you today about the tragedy of Europe. This noble continent, comprising on the whole the fairest and the most cultivated regions of the earth, enjoying a temperate and equable climate, is the home of all the great parent races of the Western world. It is the foundation of Christian faith and Christian ethics.

It is the origin of most of the culture, art, philosophy and science both of ancient and modern times. If Europe were once united in the sharing of its common inheritance there would be no limit to the happiness, the prosperity and the glory which its 300,000,000 or 400,000,000 people would enjoy. Yet it is from Europe that has sprung that series of frightful and nationalistic morals originated by the Teutonic nations in their rise to power, which we have seen in this twentieth century and which have for a long time wrecked the peace and marred the prospects of all mankind.

EUROPE SENSES NEW TERROR

And what is the plight to which Europe has been reduced? Some of the smaller states have indeed made a good recovery, but over wide areas a vast quivering mass of tormented, hungry, careworn and bewildered human beings gaze on the ruin of their cities and scan the dark horizon for the approach of some new peril, tyranny or terror.

Among the victors is a babel of voices, among the vanquished a sullen silence of despair.

That is all that Europeans, grouped in so many ancient states and nations—that is all that the Germanic races have got by tearing each other to pieces and spreading havoc far and wide. Indeed, but for the fact that the great republic across the Atlantic Ocean has at length realized that the ruin or enslavement of Europe has involved their own fate as well and has stretched out hands of succor and guidance—but for that, the Dark Ages would have returned in all their cruelty and squalor.

They may still return. There is a remedy which, if it were generally and spontaneously adopted by the great majority of people in the many lands, would, as if by a miracle, transform the whole scene and would in a few years make all Europe, or the greater part of it, as free and as happy as Switzerland is today.

A UNITED EUROPE

What is this sovereign remedy?

It is to recreate the European family, or as much of it as we can and to provide it with a structure under which it can dwell in peace, in safety and in freedom. We must build a kind of United States of Europe. In this way only will hundreds of millions of toilers be able to regain the simple joys and hopes which make life worth living.

The process is simple. All that is needed is the resolve of hundreds of millions of men and women to do right instead of wrong and to gain as their reward blessing instead of cursing. Much work has been done upon this task by the exertions of the planned European Union, which owes so much to Count Coudenhove-Calergi and which demanded the services of the famous French patron and statesman, Aristide Briand.

There is also that immense body of doctrine and procedure which was brought into being amid high hopes after the first World War. I mean the League of Nations. The League of Nations did not fail because of its principles or conceptions. It failed because these principles were deserted by those states who had brought it into being. It failed because the Governments of those days feared to face the facts and act while time remained.

This disaster must not be repeated. There is, therefore, much knowledge and material with which to build and also bitter, dear-bought experience to spur the builders.

NO CONFLICT WITH U.N.

I was very glad to read in the newspapers two days ago that my friend, President Truman, had expressed his interest and sympathy with this great design.* There is no reason why a regional organization of Europe should in any way conflict with the world organization of the United Nations.

On the contrary, I believe that the larger synthesis will only survive if it is founded upon broad natural groupings in the Western Hemisphere. We British have our own commonwealth of nations. These do not weaken—on the contrary they strengthen—the world organization. They are, in fact, its main support. And why

[* The reference is probably to remarks by Truman on September 13, 1946, at a meeting with the National Conference of Business Paper Editors where he said: "We have Government principally to act as, say, an umpire, to see that everybody gets a square deal. That is the ideal situation sought by the Constitution of the United States, which in my opinion is the greatest document the Government has ever written. It took us about 80 years to get a good start and to make it operate, and we are still trying to make it operate efficiently. I think we are gradually approaching a situation where we shall have peace in the world, with the United Nations Organization operating on the basis of a constitution for the whole world. We are going to make atomic energy a weapon of peace. We must get that mental attitude—live and let live—love one another—but then I didn't intend to preach a sermon."]

should there not be a European grouping which can give a sense of national patriotism and common citizenship to the distracted peoples of this turbulent and mighty Continent, and why should it not take its proper, rightful place, with other great groupings and help to shape the destinies of man?

In order that this may be accomplished, there must be an act of faith in which millions of families speaking many languages must consciously take part. We all know that the two world wars through which we have passed arose out of a vain passion of a newly united Germany to play a dominating part in the world. In this last struggle crimes and massacres have been committed which have no parallel since the invasion of the Mongols in the fourteenth century and have no equal at any time in human history.

BLESSED ACT OF OBLIVION

The guilty must be punished. Germany must be deprived of the power to rearm and make another aggressive war. But when all this has been done, as it will be done, as it is being done, then there must be an end to retribution.

There must be what Mr. Gladstone called a blessed act of oblivion. We must all turn our backs upon the horrors of the past. We must look to the future. We cannot afford to drag forward across the years that are to come the hatreds and revenges which have sprung from the injuries of the past.

If Europe is to be saved from infinite misery and, indeed, from final doom, there must be this act of faith in the European family and this act of oblivion against all the crimes and follies of the past, and the free peoples of Europe must rise to the height of these resolves of the soul and of the instinct of the spirit of man.

If they can, the wrongs and injuries which have been inflicted will have been washed away on all sides by the miseries which have been endured.

Is there any need for any further conflicts or agony? Is the only lesson of history to be that mankind is unteachable? Let there be justice, mercy and freedom. The people have only to will it in order to achieve their hearts' desire.

I am now going to say something that will astonish you. The first step in the re-creation of the European family must be a partnership between France and Germany.

In this way only can France recover the moral and cultural leadership of Europe.

There can be no revival of Europe without a spiritually great France and a spiritually great Germany.

The structure of the United States of Europe, if well and truly built, will be such as to make the material strength of a single state less important.

Small nations will count as much as large ones and gain their honor by their contribution to the common cause. The ancient states and principalities of Germany, newly joined together into a federal system, might take their individual place among the United States of Europe.

I shall not try to make a detailed program for hundreds of millions of people who want to be happy, free and prosperous, and wish to enjoy the four freedoms of which the great President Roosevelt spoke, and live under the principles embodied in the Atlantic Charter.

DANGERS HAVE NOT STOPPED

If this is the wish of Europeans in so many lands, then they have only to say so and means can certainly be found and machinery erected to carry that wish to full fruition. But I must give warning; time may be short. At present there may be a breathing space. The cannons have ceased firing. The fighting has stopped, but the dangers have not stopped.

If we are to form a United States of Europe, or whatever name it may take, we must begin now. In these present days we dwell strangely and precariously under the shield, and I will even say protection, of the atomic bomb. The atomic bomb is still only in the hands of a State and nation which we know will never use it except in the cause of right and freedom, but it may very well be that in a few years this awful agency of destruction will be widespread and the catastrophe following from its use by several warring nations will not only bring to an end all that we call civilization but may possibly disintegrate the globe itself.

I must now sum up the propositions which are before us. Our constant aim must be to build and fortify the strength of the United Nations organization. Under and within that world concept, we must recreate the European family in a regional structure, called, it may be, the United States of Europe, and the first practical step would be to form a Council of Europe.

If at first all states of Europe are not willing or able to join the union, we must nevertheless proceed to assemble and combine those who will and can. The salvation of the people, of the common people of every race and land, from war and servitude must be established on solid foundation and must be guarded by the readiness of all men and women to die rather than to submit to tyranny.

In all this urgent work, France and Germany must take the lead together. Great Britain, the British Commonwealth of Nations, mighty America and, I trust, Soviet Russia—and then indeed all would be well—must be the friends and sponsors of the new Europe. Let Europe arise!

Appendix G

*John Foster Dulles' Speech of January 17, 1947,
in Support of European Unity*

[*Note*: John Foster Dulles' speech of January 17, 1947, on European unity
is of interest as the first on that theme by a substantial American political
figure, for the explicitness with which it deals with the problem of
Germany in relation to European unity, and for its foreshadowing of the
critical nature of the forthcoming Moscow conference on Germany as
well as the need for increased American economic assistance to Europe
and other regions.]

"EUROPE MUST FEDERATE OR PERISH"
AMERICA MUST OFFER INSPIRATION AND GUIDANCE

By JOHN FOSTER DULLES, International Lawyer
Delivered before the National Publishers Association,
New York City, January 17, 1947

In accordance with what now is New Year's custom, we welcome
a new Secretary of State. In January, 1944, Secretary Hull held that
office; in January, 1945, it was Secretary Stettinius; in January, 1946,
it was Secretary Byrnes; now in January 1947, we have Secretary
Marshall. I first pay tribute to our retiring Secretary of State. Mr.
Byrnes, at personal risk, gallantly carried a heavy burden. His patient determination during a critical period served this nation well.
It is unfortunate that he could not carry on. Since he could not, it is
fortunate that his successor is one whose ability and character have
won for him the respect not only of the American people but of the
peoples of all the United Nations. We can hope that his great talents

which helped to fashion victory will now equally help to fashion a just and durable peace.

Republicans do not yet have title to Federal appointive office. That gives them at least the advantage of continuity. It may, therefore, be appropriate for a Republican, who had the privilege of close co-operation with the three preceding Secretaries of State, to take this occasion to look back in order the better to look forward.

Last year had some good aspects. There receded a serious risk that the victorious war coalition might break up and its members fight among themselves. It did not end the bid of the Soviet Union for world leadership. That was hardly to be expected. But 1946 did see that bid deflected into channels more compatible with peace.

DOUBLE SOVIET CHALLENGE

The Soviet challenge is double-barreled. One barrel aims at social revolution throughout the world. The other barrel aims at nationalistic expansion. The war made both targets easier to hit. Economic misery, the by-product of war, bred radical agitation throughout the world. The military position of Russia, as the great land power next to Germany and Japan, gave Soviet leadership unique opportunities to bargain for an expansion of their national domain. It is the latter type of aggressiveness which was checked in 1946 when it had already gone so far that persistence would have jeopardized the peace.

Soviet national expansion was going ahead in a big way at the end of 1945. It had begun under the cover of deals with Hitler. With his tacit acquiescence or explicit approval, part of Finland, all of Estonia, Latvia and Lithuania and large portions of Poland and Romania were incorporated into the Soviet Union. That was the price of Soviet neutrality while Hitler was attacking in the west. When Hitler turned east to attack Russia, that made Russia an ally of Britain and the United States. It was vital that the war unity of these three should be preserved, and Soviet leadership relied on that to bargain at Moscow, Teheran, Yalta and Potsdam. As a result, Soviet land power was further extended in Europe and into the Pacific.

After hostilities ended, the Soviet leaders sought to go on with their nationalistic bargaining. The first occasion was the first meeting of the Council of Foreign Ministers at London in the fall of 1945.

That conference ended with no agreement. It was publicly proclaimed a failure. It was, indeed, a failure from the standpoint of the Soviet Union. It marked the end of the ability of the Soviet Union to expand by bargaining with great powers at the expense of the weak. American idealism had a rebirth. Perhaps it would be more accurate to say that our idealism, always latent, could then safely emerge from the recesses into which it had been driven by war necessity. From then on, as Secretary Byrnes well put it, the United States might compromise within principle, but it would no longer compromise principle itself.

SOVIET EXPANSION HALTED

That was the spirit of 1946. It enabled the United States delegation through patient firmness to obtain peace treaties with Italy and the satellites which, while not ideal, involve no flagrant new injustices. More important, it halted the Soviet program of expanding at the expense of weak neighbors.

When Soviet leaders discovered, at the end of 1945, that they could no longer get our agreement to further expansion, their first reaction had been to go it alone. At the beginning of 1946, Iran, Turkey, and Greece were threatened. The result, however, was not a Soviet success. Throughout the world, public opinion reacted adversely. Soviet leaders found that they could not fire both barrels at once. Nationalistic aggression canceled out idealistic propaganda. As against that loss, there was no compensating gain, for Soviet aggressiveness had provoked in the United States and Great Britain a stronger resistance than Soviet leadership cared to face.

In these countries public opinion quickly hardened. It supported measures to rebuild military establishments which had been allowed to disintegrate. The United States displayed naval and air power in the Mediterranean. It seemed that if the Soviet continued along the line upon which it had embarked, that might even lead to major war. That is one thing which Soviet leadership does not now want and would not consciously risk. Economically the nation is still weak in consequence of war devastation. Also, for the time being, the Soviet military establishment is completely outmatched by the mechanized weapons—particularly the atomic weapons—available to the United States.

REALISTIC LEADERSHIP

So, as competent observers had thought likely, Soviet leaders drew back. That is to their credit. Soviet leadership showed itself to be intelligent and realistic rather than reckless or fanatical. That is a reassuring fact, because often leaders who are dynamic and who have had great initial successes become over-confident. They take ever greater risks until they find to their chagrin that they have made a bad calculation and have precipitated trouble which they never wanted or expected. The Politburo, at least in 1946, did not go down that path.

The greatest credit for the 1946 result goes to the American people. They quickly cleared their minds of war romanticism which had overidealized all of the Allies and their objectives. They were able to see realities even when they were unpleasant realities, and, despite post-war weariness, they hardened their wills. There were a few who were gullible and who still believed, because Soviet leadership used idealism as propaganda, that that leadership itself was idealistic. But they were only a small and ineffectual minority. The American people showed that they still possessed to a high degree the ability to see clearly and to think straight.

Bi-partisan co-operation played an important part in the result. Governor Dewey, during the campaign of 1944, agreed with President Roosevelt that there should be a permanent world organization. That act made logical a bi-partisan delegation to the San Francisco conference. That worked so well that Secretary Byrnes invited Republicans to participate in negotiating the first group of peace treaties and to participate in the Assembly of the United Nations. Thus Democrats and Republicans sat side by side, and we both learned, at the same time and from the same bench, as it were, some of the hard facts of international life. That learning together is the key to effective bi-partisanship. In this case it made it natural that Democratic leadership through Secretary Byrnes and Republican leadership through Senator Vandenberg should speak to the American people in similar terms. That contributed greatly to solidifying the American attitude.

Credit goes to the United Nations. Its open processes were what made it impracticable for Soviet leadership to play, at the same time, incompatible roles. It compelled choice between idealistic propaganda in non-contiguous lands and hardboiled militarism toward neighboring countries. It enabled world opinion to register and show the expediency of the more peaceful course.

We can look back on 1946 with some satisfaction. But it should only be satisfaction that a long, hard task has been well begun. If 1946 saw the Soviet nationalistic challenge become less aggressive, we cannot assume that even that phase is definitely over. Certainly Soviet leadership does not accept as final the present status of the Dardanelles. In its other phase—the ideological phase—the Soviet challenge became increasingly powerful. In most of the world effective popular leadership is in the hands of persons who are sympathetic to Soviet Communist doctrines and who turn to Moscow for moral support.

In India, Soviet Communism exercises a strong influence through the interim Hindu government.

In China, United States efforts to end the civil war have collapsed, and Communist forces hopefully continue their struggle.

COLONIAL REBELLION

Throughout the colonial areas there is growing rebellion against the white man's assumption of racial superiority. The fighting now going on in Dutch Indonesia and in French Indo-China is symptomatic of a widespread condition. These revolutionary movements are encouraged by Soviet leadership which pretends to a "classless" society.

The Arab world grows increasingly hostile as the strain regarding Palestine is prolonged.

In Latin America Communist leaders are steadily gaining in political power. They are effectively agitating against the so-called "capitalism" and "imperialism" of the United States. Hemispheric solidarity is precarious and the Monroe Doctrine faces its sternest test.

In western Europe Communist strength has grown so that in France and Italy Communists now exercise a large measure of governmental power.

In the United States Soviet leaders look to "boom-bust" finally to discredit capitalism and to liquidate the last vestiges of our claim to economic supremacy. That collapse, they profess, is inevitable.

However, they deem it prudent to help the inevitable, and to this end their followers have burrowed into the core of our economic body.

PRESSURE TO DISARM

At the recent "town meeting of the world" the Soviet delegation achieved a large measure of leadership. Also, they there did an effective job in portraying the United States as militaristic and imperialistic. They persuaded many that this nation ought to disarm itself in the interest of world peace. Soviet leaders hope thus to end the military inequality which bothered them in 1946.

Those are some of the items of the 1946 heritage with which 1947 must deal. It is a heritage which is hailed joyfully by the new year's press of the Soviet Union. It is, for us, a heritage to be accepted with soberness. It does not contain immediate danger, as did the heritage of 1945, but it does threaten us with an isolation which sooner or later would gravely endanger us. Also, it is a form of challenge which is difficult to meet. In 1946 our foreign policy had two main elements, negation toward Soviet expansion and relief of those suffering privation. In 1947 we shall still need the ability to say "no." We shall still need to provide some relief. But we shall need more than that. Negation is never a permanent substitute for creation, and no nation is so poor as a nation which can give only dollars. The need is for spiritual and intellectual vigor and the leadership which that bestows.

Today most of the peoples of the world find their established institutions swept away. They must build anew. One hundred years ago, fifty years ago, they would have looked to us for inspiration and guidance, and they would not have looked in vain. They must not now look to us in vain. Let that be our New Year's resolve.

THE MOSCOW CONFERENCE

The forthcoming Moscow conference will show whether we have the wisdom to prescribe healing of such vast dislocations as everywhere surround us. That conference will deal with Germany. Whoever deals with Germany deals with the central problem of Europe. Whoever deals with Europe deals with the world's worst fire hazard. Repeatedly it bursts out in flames. Twice within the last thirty years the edifice has virtually burned to the ground. The

160

human and material losses have been colossal and irreparable. After each past conflagration the structure has been rebuilt substantially as before.

Statesmanship can do better than go on repeating that folly. The trouble is not hard to find. Our founders diagnosed the situations many years ago. Alexander Hamilton put it in these historic words:

> To look for a continuation of harmony between a number of independent, unconnected sovereignties in the same neighborhood would be to disregard the uniform course of human events and to set at defiance the accumulated experience of ages.

Not only did our founders diagnose the trouble; they found for themselves the remedy. They placed matters of concern to all under an administration responsible to all.

The war victors will do well to have that formula in mind. Then, when they plan the future of Germany, they will think more in terms of the economic unity of Europe and less in terms of the Potsdam dictum that Germany shall be "a single economic unit." Of course, there should be an economic unification of Germany. But the reason for that is also a reason for the economic unification of Europe. A Europe divided into small economic compartments cannot be a healthy Europe. All of Europe's economic potentialities need to be used and European markets should be big enough to justify modern methods of cheap production for mass consumption. That, no doubt, is why Mr. Attlee declared some time ago that "Europe must federate or perish."

Of course, the German settlement will not of itself bring about a federation of Europe. Only the European peoples themselves can do that, and they will probably move slowly. But the German settlement will decisively determine whether the movement will be toward economic unification or toward rebuilding the old structure of independent, unconnected sovereignties.

The basin of the Rhine, with its coal and industrious manpower, constitutes the natural economic heart of western Europe. From that area ought to flow vitality not merely for Germans but for Germany's western neighbors. If that happens, western Europe, at least, with its 200,000,000 people, could develop into a more prosperous and stable land. That, however, is not likely to happen if the

German peace treaty merely re-establishes Germany as a single economic unity subject to only German political control which, even if originally decentralized, could again become highly centralized.

FEAR OF GERMAN RISE

If such dispositions are made, Germany's western neighbors—France, Belgium and Holland—will hesitate to organize their economies into dependence on a source which may again be controlled by ambitious and vengeful German rulers. That might enable Germans hereafter to achieve, by economic pressures, a mastery of western Europe which they could not achieve by arms. Rather than risk that, the nations of western Europe will probably annex bits of Germany as they can and, as to the rest, accept economic separation. That would condemn western Europe to an unhealthy and precarious existence.

Not only is such a solution bad for Europe; it is bad for peace. If the industrial potential of western Germany cannot safely be integrated into western Europe, it ought not to be fully used by Germans alone. It is then logical to impose what the Potsdam declaration calls "industrial disarmament." That is another word for pastoralization. Its inevitable accompaniment is military occupation and charity feeding. Actually no one of those three elements can have permanency. Not only Germans but neighboring peoples will eventually rebel at trying to cover with manure the natural industrial basin of Europe.

Peace-time armies of occupation are a tremendous moral hazard to themselves and to others, and, while long-term military guaranties as proposed by Senator Vandenberg will be required, the American people will not indefinitely keep in Germany the huge armies which would be needed to repress restless people deprived of the work for which they are fitted. Also, the American people will not indefinitely provide immense charity to prevent mass starvation which threatens only because artificial conditions are imposed.

DECENTRALIZATION NEEDED

Peace should not be made dependent upon artificial conditions which hold only so long as there is external coercion. That was the main trouble with the Treaty of Versailles. Its terms, if enforced, would have kept Germany impotent for a thousand years. But enforcement depended upon external coercion, which rapidly evaporated. Peace conditions, to be durable, should be self-enforcing. What is needed in respect of Germany is decentralization, at the beginning, that can be imposed. A large measure of political autonomy can be given to German states. But that decentralization will not stick unless also there develop natural forces which turn the inhabitants of Germany's states toward their outer neighbors. The economic forces operating upon Germans should be centrifugal and not centripetal. Only if decentralization is enforced by such forces can it be depended upon.

When the German problem is thus analyzed, it is apparent that it calls for some application of the federal formula. Under our federal system the citizens of Pennsylvania share with others legislative control over the interstate movement of their coal and their steel products. The Port of New York is operated by an autonomous authority established by treaty between New Jersey and New York. The Tennessee Valley development is operated by a Federal authority, not by the state of Tennessee. We propose an international authority to own and operate atomic development everywhere so that nowhere can it fall under national control which might use it for war rather than for economic welfare.

Such precedents suggest that it is not beyond human resourcefulness to find a form of joint control which will make it possible to develop the industrial potential of western Germany in the interest of the economic life of western Europe, including Germany, and do so without making Germans the masters of Europe.

HELP FROM AMERICA

Whether a solution along this line is practical, and the scope to be given it, will depend primarily upon our Continental allies themselves. The non-Continental victors—Soviet Russia, Great Britain and the United States—cannot impose any such solution. If, however, our Continental friends are thinking constructively—and there is evidence that many of them are—we Americans ought to be able to give them precious assistance. We possess, with Great Britain, decisive power in Western Germany. We have, more than any other people, experience in using the federal formula and in developing its manifold possibilities. If we employ these assets to solve the problem of Germany, we shall have made a good start in implementing our 1947 resolve.

I have spoken particularly of Europe. But I did so only by way of illustration, and not with any thought that we can safely concentrate on one part of the world to the neglect of the rest. Not only in Europe, but in Asia, South America and the colonial areas, there are vast tasks of reconstruction to be undertaken. Old societies need to be rebuilt. Sick societies need to be made well. Societies subject to alien rule need peaceful roads to freedom. We should become again, as we once were, the source to which men turn for inspiration and guidance in the accomplishment of such tasks.

We Americans believe that our individualistic society best qualifies men for leadership. Such a society, we believe, provides the richness of diversity and of experimentation and the stimulus of competition. That, I say, is our belief. But it is no longer the belief of others. They are skeptical. They are frightened by the unruly aspect we present, and they suspect us of a certain moral and intellectual bankruptcy. They are attracted by the apparent smoothness and efficiency of a society where conformity is the rule and where all men walk in step. That is why Soviet Communism can seriously challenge us for world leadership. The time has come when we shall have to put up or shut up.

I am confident that out of the physical vigor of our people and the intellectual stimulus of our free society can come the constructive ideas for which the whole world stands in wait. If it does come, we shall again be safe, for we shall have given leadership, and in return, we shall receive fellowship.

Appendix H

Memorandum of March 26, 1946,
by a Member of EUR, David Harris,
Arguing for U.S. Support for German Unity

[*Note*: This thoughtful memorandum is of interest because its author was a member of EUR who advocated a more active U.S. policy in support of German unity as of March 26, 1946. I do not recall whether Harris also supported our plan for an all-European settlement in circulation at the time he wrote this memorandum; but, since he worked in the highly disciplined structure of EUR, within the Division of Central European Affairs (CE), he may have thought it inappropriate to comment on GA's unorthodox proposal for an all-European settlement.]

TO: CE—Mr. Riddleberger   DATE: March 26, 1946
         EUR—Mr. Matthews
FROM: CE—David Harris
SUBJECT: Future Policy toward Germany

Need for New Statement of Policy: The purpose of this memorandum is to examine the problem of future policy toward Germany. The present governing document (JCS 1067 and IPCOG 1/4, May 11, 1945) states: "This directive sets forth policies relating to Germany in the initial post-defeat period. As such it is not intended to be an ultimate statement of policies of this Government concerning the treatment of Germany in the post-war world."

To a considerable degree the provisions of that interim directive have been effected in the United States zone of occupation, although relatively little has been accomplished under the instruction, "As a member of the Control Council you will urge the adoption by the other occupying powers of the principles and policies set forth in this directive. . . ."

By reason of the extensive accomplishment in the United States zone and the meager accomplishment in terms of Germany as a whole, it seems to me that the time is now at hand to consider the kind of program which should be adopted for the next period of the occupation of Germany. A statement of long-range objectives and the means for reaching them is all the more desirable in view of the problem posed by the present French position, a problem which can not be easily or wisely resolved without a fairly clear sense of what we desire with respect to Germany in the long run. Likewise the energetic role of the Soviet authorities counsels a review of our intentions.

The Present Trend toward Partition: The first problem, as I see it, is whether we wish to maintain the assumption of the Potsdam Declaration that Germany should remain a single state.

The present tendency in Germany is toward effective partition. Soviet Military Government last autumn organized a so-called Central Administration for the Soviet zone and this Administration seems progressively to be curtailing the wide autonomy originally granted the provincial and *Land* authorities by Marshal Zhukov. In the United States zone the *Laenderrat* was planned as a conference of the three ministers-president which would merely coordinate administration on an advisory basis in the three *Laender* but, in spite of the announced intention to the contrary, the German bureaucracy growing in numbers and functions at Stuttgart is certainly becoming a central German government for the United States zone. The British have not advanced as far along the road of administrative reorganization but zone-wide *ad hoc* economic organizations and other activities point definitely in the same direction. Regardless of political intentions, current economic necessities are forcing a consolidation of functions on a level higher than the individual province or *Land.*

There is only one way to reverse this tendency—the establishment of the central administrative agencies envisaged at Potsdam.

But do we wish, in the light of what appears to be current developments, to reverse our previous position and allow the division between eastern and western Germany to perpetuate itself?

Policies of the Other Occupying Powers: In seeking an answer one might try to fix in mind as clear a picture of the policies of the other three Occupying Powers as possible.

1. *Soviet Policy*: I have tried to be extremely cautious in assaying the Soviet policy but I conclude that the Soviet Government is intent on a Communist Germany perhaps for reasons of dogma as well as for the practical reason of having a Germany in close alliance with, or dependent on, Russia. The original program last year of a close union of all "anti-fascist" parties was tentative and not altogether honest. It is generally understood that the authorization to form a second "bourgeois" party—and the authorization really meant an order—was inspired by the desire to split the ranks of non-Marxists between the Christian Democratic Union and the Liberal Democratic Party. In the beginning each of the four authorized parties was permitted to set up a newspaper in Berlin on terms of equality one with another, but the fiction of equality was abandoned soon by giving the Communist Party paper the lion's share of the essential materials. The *Land* reform program in the Soviet zone led to a not very skillful mutiny on the part of the Christian Democrats against the unstable union of the four parties and the way in which Marshal Zhukov in person raked Hermes over the coals for hours at a time and finally had him removed by a synthetic rebellion of Christian Democrats proved very clearly that political parties could function in the Soviet zone only as long as they accepted Communist leadership and Soviet direction.

At the same time, however, the Hermes crisis and the qualified subservience of Kaiser, his successor, undoubtedly indicated that the United Front would not work well as the instrument for conducting the social revolution which is already under way in the Soviet zone. And too, the United Front was actually non-existent in the West where the Americans, the British and the French had no intention of coercing nascent political activity into that mold. The Communist Party, however, was too weak and too embarrassed by its Russian connections to undertake the revolution alone. Hence the device of a union of the two Marxist parties. Since their internecine quarrels have been clearly recognized as one of the means whereby "fascism" came to power, there is undeniably a logic for the Left in union, and the Communists have made the most of it. It was equally obvious, however, that logic would not persuade the Social Democrats overnight and so the present *Sozialistische Einheitspartei Deutschlands* is again a product of Soviet intimidation. A recent report of a meeting in Berlin indicates that, even there where the Russian hand is heavy, there is strong resistance to the union, but, in so far as I can foresee, the Russians really have no other political alternative and must stick to and push the amalgamated party. German Communism and ergo the new party are so obviously tarred with the Soviet brush that it will be a long time before the movement can regain its pre-war dimensions in Germany—unless conditions are such that Communism becomes a plausible way out, in spite of its Soviet connections.

Meanwhile the Soviet authorities are not only using the services of the German Communists but are busy, with still some inconsistencies of conduct, in attempting to secure a more friendly attitude on the part of the whole populace of their zone. The Communist and Red Army overt newspapers have been presenting daily under big headlines the economic recovery of the Soviet zone and the end of factory requisitions. A less subtle form of good-will building was the distribution of coal to every resident of the Soviet sector of Berlin in November and December, in contravention of Kommandatura agreement. I have seen a copy of a Christmas card which was sent, I am told, in wholesale lots from Soviet military government officials to influential Germans; the general burden of it was: "I wish you a very Merry Christmas and foresee through our united efforts a happier day to come."

In the same vein, Kaiser and Lemmer, first and second leaders of the CDU respectively, told me of repeated assurances from the Russians that the Oder-Neisse line was not definitive; where the German frontier would eventually be fixed depended entirely on the Germans. The other day when Ulbricht, nominally the deputy but actually the principal leader of the Communists, made his opening salvo against division he referred to the unity of Germany except *Silesia*; certainly by implication he means the return of the northern areas east of the Oder and certainly he would not have so described his exception without Soviet approval. In short, the Russians, to supplement the force exerted through the Communist Party, are offering the German people as a whole attractive rewards, some tangible and some intangible, for their cooperation.

In the meanwhile the Soviet authorities are confronted with the question of the projected central German agencies and the French demands with respect to the Rhineland and the Ruhr. As the matter now stands the Russians are committed to the central agencies and they have allowed, as noted, the German Communists to champion national unity while, contrariwise, they have allowed the French Communists to take a stand in direct opposition to that of their German comrades. Ambassador Murphy in his 602 of February 24 and Mr. Kennan in his 672 of March 6 have considered this general situation. The Ambassador points to the capital which the Communists are making out of their championship of opposition to the French proposals and wishes that pressure be put on the Paris Government to secure agreement on the central agencies in order to combat the favorable position which this recent development has given the Soviet authorities and the Communist Party and in order also to attack the exclusive Soviet control of such a large part of Germany.

Mr. Kennan is more definitely convinced than is Ambassador Murphy that the disparity of views between German and French Communists is of Kremlin manufacture and he sees the Russians content to have the French receive the onus for holding up the central agencies while the Red Army consolidates its position in the Soviet zone. The attitude which the Russians ultimately will take toward the central agencies, Mr. Kennan believes, will depend on their judgment as to what will best forward their program of an "anti-Fascist Republic;" should they consider the central agencies useful they will instruct Thorez to modify his nationalistic stand.

With respect to the Rhineland and the Ruhr, Mr. Kennan believes that the Russians are carrying water on both shoulders until the future is clearer. In the end they might be guided by their decision as to which Communist Party, the German or the French, would best serve their ends. At the same time Mr. Kennan sees the Russians prepared to move in response to the moves of the Western Powers. If we support a united Germany and, by our relative neutrality in internal politics, give the Communists a chance to win, the Russians will undoubtedly press, in Mr. Kennan's judgment, for unity; if, on the other hand, the Western Powers independently set about integrating their zones into the Western pattern of economy, the Soviet Government would come out for an internationalized Ruhr and an independent Rhineland. By the context, I take it, Mr. Kennan envisages in this case a scheme of internationalization in which the Soviet Union would have appropriate representation.

2. *French Policy*: The French Government appears to have com-

bined a fear of Russian power on the Rhine with their old apprehension of Germany and, apparently, will continue to espouse the present program of annexation and occupation until coerced or beguiled by concessions elsewhere into accepting another plan. Under any circumstances it is to be assumed that the French will put up a vigorous fight for permanent possession of the Saar and for a long-term occupation of much of the Rhineland.

3. *British Policy*: The British Government is seemingly pursuing a policy of watchful waiting. Feeling a need for close ties on the continent, it would prefer to give the support of Britain to France but since it has doubts as to the ability of the French to regain its status as genuinely a Great Power, it is unwilling at this time to give the *coup de grâce* to the possibility of reviving Germany as a friendly force in the uncertain world of the future. A more immediate concern for London is, of course, the critical food shortage in the British zone. Hardly less critical is the need for getting the industry of Western Germany functioning to take care of necessities beyond this immediate crisis. We can anticipate, therefore, that the British will actively support the creation of the projected central agencies and will wish to restore a functioning economic unit in Germany. The only hesitation would arise if there were clear prospect that Germany was going Communist.

With respect to Western Germany, the Foreign Office in February was well advanced with a paper which would propose an economic control of the Ruhr without political separation from Germany (London Embassy telegram No. 1752, February 12). It is a plan, I judge, which would give some need of satisfaction to France but which would, at the same time, preserve the basic integrity of Germany west of the Oder-Neisse line.

Prospective German Reactions: The next consideration to be raised by this memorandum involves future German reactions. There are, in my opinion, two critical questions which require discussion.

1. *Possibility of Communism*: The first question is whether Germany will turn Communist. There is no doubt that Soviet pressure is in that direction. The Party has the open support of the Soviet occupation authorities and numerous inducements are being held out to individual Germans to join the Party. Present Party membership includes the following types of persons:

(a) Old-time Party men who kept the faith during the Hitler regime; many of them were able to do so by flight to Russia and long residence there. Pieck and Ulbricht, the two leaders, belong to this category.

(b) Younger men for the most part, who were indoctrinated in the Soviet Union after capture as prisoners of war.

(c) Certain persons coerced into the Party in order to save their jobs or their property.

(d) Opportunists who have joined for material advantages or because the Party with its undercurrent of violence and irrationality offered psychological satisfactions.

These categories comprise the major membership up to the present time. Three or four other groups are potentially large-scale sources of Party strength.

(a) Possibly a certain number of the younger generation of the trade union movement who will be swept in by the vigor and the strong organization which the Communists show in labor problems.

(b) Former Nazis, most of whom played such inconspicuous roles in the NSDAP as to escape the usual penalties. The Communist Party offers several varieties of former Nazis much of the same emotional bait which took them into Hitler's organizations. One has but to listen to the Soviet-controlled radio, attend a rally, or read a Communist paper to sense the strong common denominator of the two parties. At the present time the Communists are beginning to open their rosters to the little Pg's on the very plausible ground that the little Pg's are salvageable material. I am persuaded that a great horde of ex-Nazis will find their new home in the Communist Party, and notably so if the Party can arrogate to itself the legacy of Hitler's nationalism.

(c) Nationalists and militarists in general provided developing circumstances allow the Communists to make plausible pretensions to being special custodians of German unity and German honor. There were many German patriots who threw their support to Hitler in spite of various otherwise repugnant aspects of National Socialism because the Nazis did promise a national resurrection, and it may be anticipated that these same people will not be too squeamish about the bandwagon on which they ride so long as it goes in the direction of patriotism. The militarists—defined for this purpose as professional soldiers, and particularly those who have General Staff mentality—constitute good human material for indoctrination. As a group they have nothing in common with the liberal rational tradition of the West. Authoritarianism and unquestioning service are virtues of high appeal to them. There is an old history of cordiality between German and Russian officers, a newer history of close relations in the Weimar period, and a still newer history of the organization of prisoners in Russia. Certain of the officers involved in the abortive Putsch of July 20, 1944 had a rather mystic idea about the Soviet Union and looked forward to a close association of the two countries. The officer class is now without professional occupation and the proud bearing of officers now enrolling in the universities indicates that they are a very dangerous element in the German population, an element which may embrace any cause as long as it has a nationalistic coloring.

(d) A final category of potential Communists is the most obvious one—the league of the desperate who will be prepared in case of prolonged economic distress to follow any piper who blows a loud tune.

On the other side of the scale of Germany's political future there is a heavy weight against Communism.

(a) The fears of the propertied classes need no special mention.

(b) Nor does the hostility of the average peasant. It might only be pointed out that perhaps the one politically significant fact of the January elections in the smaller communities of the United States zone was the wide-spread determination to roll up a large vote against Communism in order to set a precedent for the future. Among others who spoke to me of this attitude was the Minister-President of Baden-Wuerttemberg.

(c) Equally obvious is the opposition of the religious forces of both creeds. The organization of the Christian Democratic Union and the Bavarian Christian Socialist Union gives promise of providing a more effective vehicle for the exertion of Christian influence on political life than was the case under the Weimar Constitution.

(d) The Social Democrats are going to be badly split by the Soviet pressure to amalgamate but it is safe to say that the Russian haste has alienated a number of Social Democrats who might have supported union had they been given time to debate the issue freely in a national party conference. I talked with several party leaders who took this position. The Social Democrats in Berlin, and even in the Soviet zone, put on a remarkable display of civic courage recently in a stormy conference and the leaders from the West are uncompromisingly hostile to union on the present terms of equality of the two parties. The mass of the Social Democrats, consequently, may be counted on for continuing opposition to Communism.

(e) Likewise the trade unions as a workers' movement over Germany as a whole will probably resist Communist attempts at domination for as long as there is any reasonable hope of victory.

These groups constitute an overwhelming majority of the German population and they will have on their side an ancient popular prejudice against the Slavs which was fanned into fanaticism by the Nazis and which had seemingly a powerful confirmation in the conduct of the Russian soldatesca in Germany.

Yet the question remains, can these anti-Communists, anti-Soviet forces hold their line against the enormous pressure which is being exerted and which probably will grow in violence? My own conviction is that they will—provided the economic and moral situation does not become so wretched that they will, like the drowning man clutching at the serpent, embrace Communism and the blandishments held out by the Soviet Union.

The economic proviso needs no elaborate gloss. The existing fact is a Germany divested of the agricultural and industrial resources east of the Oder-Neisse line, crippled by air attacks and land fighting and removal of industry in the name of war booty and reparation, inundated by several million destitute refugees from neighboring lands, and, finally, torn into four virtually airtight regions. And, on top of such misfortunes, the populace is faced with a reduction of food to a dangerously low and, indeed, starvation level. The sum total of these disasters means as hopeless a nation as one can imagine. And hopelessness, I have tried to indicate above, is the best seed bed that can be devised for Communism in Germany.

The task of doing something about this situation is a formidable one, and made all the more so, as Mr. Kennan and others have long since recognized, by the loss of the regions east of the Oder-Neisse line. Because of this loss and because of the influx of refugees, Germany has been made more clearly than ever dependent on external relations and that dependence, as present lines of economic interest are organized, must now be either on the Soviet Union or on the Western Powers. Manifestly, then, if we wish to make any effort to prevent Germany from going Communist we, along with Great Britain and France, are impelled to exert every effort to breathe new life into Germany's prostrate economy by integrating it as a prospering element, into our own.

The moral proviso may be more intangible but is, in my opinion, no less real. It involves, if one can venture to put a complex psychological problem succinctly, a hope, a prospect that Germans can be not only economically prosperous but that Germans can be admitted as equals in the society of respectable—and respected—peoples. The first practical obligation might be to examine, in the light of the past year's experience, the political effect of the war criminal trials and of our efforts to convince the population of Germany's war guilt. Without modifying in the least degree our convictions of Germany's guilt, the question can well be asked if our treatment of this question has attained in Germany the results we desired.

2. *German Attitude toward Partition*: The second of the fundamental questions concerning Germany is whether it would be possible in the long run to effect one of the alternatives suggested by Mr. Kennan, viz., "to carry to its logical conclusion the process of partition which was begun in the east and endeavor to rescue Western zones of Germany by walling them off against eastern penetration and integrating them into international pattern of western Europe rather than into a united Germany."

An attempt to this end would require first that the French give up the Byzantine complexities of their scheme for the Rhineland and the Ruhr and that every effort be made to develop the economic possibilities of this half of Germany as an integral part of western economy. The first qualification would be that western economy, if there be a functioning unity bearing that name, would be in a position to absorb the German economy by providing necessary markets for exports and by sending the necessary imports of goods and capital. Without large supplies of capital the venture would most certainly be doomed to failure. This process of rehabilitation would need to be carried forward much more rapidly in the case of a partitioned western Germany than in the case of Germany as a whole in order to meet the competition of the eastern Communists and their Soviet supporters, and it would encounter far greater difficulties than if the old organic structure of Germany were dealt with.

The prospect of integrating the western half of Germany into a revived international liberal system in sufficient time and on a sufficient scale of prosperity to give the populace a tolerable standard of living is so meager that, whatever the alternative, the attempt can hardly be considered as anything more than an act of desperation.

Yet even supposing that a relatively successful economic reorganization took place in Western Germany, it is necessary to inquire whether partition could be maintained without a lasting coercion which would require an impractically expensive military force with all of its attendant dangers. Or, to state the question in another way, would a fairly decent standard of living and a fear of Communism lead the Germans of the West to abandon their pre-war devotion to national unity and accept dismemberment?

As an initial observation it must be noted that the war and the rigors of this first post-war year have not revealed a genuine rift in the old national feeling which could be exploited for purposes of an East-West separation. The few minute ripples in the waters of *Deutschtum* along the western frontier have been largely the work of foreign agents and there is no basis for supposing that separatism in that region could command any serious public sympathy. The recent manifestations of provincialism in Bavaria, in turn, are of no significance for the question under examination. The Bavarian movement is in large measure a synthetic affair with a bit of the ironic in it since it is directed by an old-time Social Democrat who is so opportunistic as not only to go back on his Party's traditional centralist policy but also to attend Catholic services every Sunday. But even in so far as Bavarian particularism is real it would be directed as much against a close organization of western Germany as against a united Germany.

Any answer to the question of whether food would be an acceptable substitute for national unity can only be a surmise but, in the light of the clear pages of recent German history, the safest surmise is that it would not. My most sober conviction is that restoration of German unity would be the major preoccupation of the German people on both sides of a partition line and that, consequently, the Occupying Powers and the world at large would have no respite until that objective was attained. It is equally my sober judgment that if the people of western Germany became convinced that Communism offered the best means of unity, the majority of them would become Communist. The outspoken French position together with American and British silence on the issue have already given the Communists their opportunity to pose as champions of the principal issue in German life and people who stomached National Socialism on patriotic grounds will not be immune to the pretensions of Communism. I conclude, therefore, that the most certain way of making Western Germany Communist is to try to bar the road to Communism by partitioning Germany.

Conditions for Success of a Policy based on German Unity: One must, however, weigh with scrupulous care the conditions for success in continuing a policy based on German unity.

As has been suggested above, the British would probably cooperate, the French would perhaps at best be an unwilling partner and the Russians would help or hinder as the interests of Communism would dictate. But since the Russians will be working for the interest of Communism in either case, the question is one again of how best to contest the expansion of this doctrine. And that question poses the further question of how best to assist non-Communist Germans to control their country, because the issue is going to be decided at the critical moment by the Germans, not by ourselves.

By an emphatic stand in favor of German national unity we would take from the hands of the Communists a dangerous weapon. Yet without a vigorous positive policy this purely negative stand will have little ultimate value. This vigorous positive policy must be based on the reasoned assessment of what is needed in Germany in order to achieve the aim of halting the march of Communism; it means, if it is to be effective, an abandonment of the vindictiveness which has frequently colored our policy toward Germany through the workings of justified anger at the barbarities and obscenities of a Nazified nation.

Before going on, however, it would be in order to note what a positive policy should not mean. It should not mean—to touch my last observation first—it should not mean forgiving or forgetting the bad things which the Germans have perpetrated; it should not mean sentimentality of any kind for sentimentality would be no sounder basis for a constructive policy than would the eye-for-an-eye fury of a man who wanted to flood the coal mines of the Ruhr.

A positive policy, further, should not mean overlooking reasonable disarmament and security precautions and should, above all things, not mean rebuilding the military power of Germany as a counter-balance to Russian might. This last point I assume to be axiomatic, but I should like to emphasize the conviction that there is no incompatibility between an intelligently planned and administered program of German rehabilitation on the one hand and security on the other. Security has been complicated by persons who at times either disguise or rationalize their vindictiveness and by persons who fear the victors' ability to enforce disarmament and, in an illogical anxiety, wish to multiply controls until the whole system is bound to break down. The problem is relatively simple: Germany without trained men and weapons cannot fight. If we cannot enforce those prohibitions no others would be enforceable; if we can, no others are necessary.

Principles of a Constructive Program: The principles forming the basis of a constructive program seem to me to be the following:

1. A governmental reconstruction of Germany as a whole which would give the central administrative agencies adequate powers to cope with the legitimate social and economic problems of the contemporary state. A state so decentralized that it is too weak to meet legitimate national needs is certain to be repudiated by the people who are victims of its incapacity. That a vigorous effort in this direction is an immediate imperative of United States policy I assume requires no further demonstration or argument.

2. An equally vigorous economic program designed (a) to give effect to the agreed plan of treating Germany as an economic entity, (b) to reconstruct legitimate German industry, (c) to reorganize the financial system, (d) to integrate reviving German economy into world trade. A corollary of such a program would be a definitive clarification of the reparation problem as quickly as possible. While the western part of Germany remains confused, the Russians are winning applause because of the alleged halt to removals from the Soviet zone. Such a program need not sacrifice the principle of preferential treatment to European members of the United Nations; it would simply mean recognition of the inescapable fact that Europe cannot be prosperous unless Germany is a successful economic constituent.

3. A propaganda campaign the core of which is the assurance that

a Germany which sets its political and moral house in order can earn an honorable place in the society of nations. Such a campaign must look forward rather than backward. It involves cleaning up the war-criminal business as quickly as possible and making prompt disposition of the people now in prison camps as a result of action under the automatic arrest clauses.

4. A parallel propaganda campaign on the meaning of democracy. The word has recently been so prostituted that it is distasteful to millions of Germans, but we could, I believe, restore meaning to it by an energetic reiteration of our view that democracy means respect for human dignity and intellectual and moral freedom.

5. A fifth point which concerns the United States exclusively is painful to set down on paper yet it is essential if we are to exercise the influence in Germany which we should exercise in the interest of the foregoing principles. It is simply that there should be a marked improvement in the conduct of United States personnel in Germany, an improvement which should be sought by imposing better discipline and by an educational program to give our troops a knowledge of what our policy is and some clearer sense of their responsibility for it.

These principles, I recognize, suffer under the obvious limitation of being vague generalities, but I believe they state the point of view and constitute the basis of more detailed planning which are the essential predicates for a constructive program. The crisis of our presence in Germany and of the future of the German people cannot be adequately attacked by a tinkering with JCS 1067. It must be met, in my judgment, by formulating a clear notion of long-range intentions and then building an immediate practical program to give effect to them.

By adopting such principles and setting to work to give them practical effect we would be exposing ourselves to no serious risk. Drifting from one *ad hoc* expedient to another, especially at a time when the economic situation is so bad and when the German people are rapidly recovering from the shock of their experiences, can only drive Germany more rapidly down the road to Communism. *Concluding Proposal*: I should like to propose, consequently, that a new statement of policy be prepared without delay in the Department of State under the chairmanship of the Division of Central

European Affairs and that this policy be submitted to the State-War-Navy Coordinating Committee for transmission through appropriate channels to the Commander-in-Chief of the United States forces in the European Theater.

DAVID HARRIS

Notes

1. Press references to the Acheson-Clayton proposal are given in Note 3, below, their texts in Appendix B. Documentary references to the Acheson-Clayton plan are found in the lengthy telegrams regarding the German problem which Acheson and John Hilldring sent to Secretary Byrnes at the Paris Foreign Ministers conference on May 9, 1946 (740.00119 Control [Germany]/5-946 [reproduced as Appendix C]); in a memo from Charles P. Kindleberger to Benjamin Cohen (April 5, 1946) warning of an impending European split unless the United States launched a diplomatic offensive to prevent it (pp. 60–62, above); and in a memo from W. W. Rostow to Herbert Marks (April 8, 1946) regarding ESP's position opposing French proposals for the detachment of the Ruhr and Rhineland (740.00119 Control [Germany]/4-846). Attached to the Rostow memo was a draft of the all-European settlement proposal that Acheson and Clayton eventually presented to Byrnes in late April. An earlier draft of that proposal, together with a favorable cover memo from Emilio Collado, had been sent to Clayton on February 26, 1946, and is included in Appendix A. The memorandum from James Riddleberger to the senior officials of the State Department of March 19, 1946, reporting the combined staff view on the French Rhineland-Ruhr proposals notes: "ESP concurs in this recommendation but has attached a separate statement . . . recommending that the negotiation of the French proposal for the separation of the Ruhr and Rhineland be made the occasion for a major diplomatic offensive by the United States

designed to halt and reverse the present movement toward an exclusive bloc structure in Europe."

An April 12, 1946, letter from Columbia University economics professor James Angell to Byrnes (740.00119 Council/4-1246) expressed strong support for a comprehensive European settlement and noted that "a more detailed development" of ideas for an American initiative along those lines had been "worked out in rough preliminary form by Mr. Clayton and his staff." A brief summary of the plan and W. W. Rostow's role in its formulation can be found in Charles P. Kindleberger's July 22, 1948, Memorandum for the Files, "Origins of the Marshall Plan," *Foreign Relations of the United States, 1947* (Washington, D.C.: Government Printing Office, 1969), vol. 3, pp. 241–247.

Few secondary works on American foreign policy mention the Acheson-Clayton plan. David Wightman, *Economic Cooperation in Europe: A Study of the United Nations Economic Commission for Europe* (New York: Frederick A. Praeger, 1956), pp. 17–19, cites the proposal in some detail, attributing it to "younger officials in the State Department." Probably the most accurate reference to the plan and its formulation is in Max Beloff, *The United States and the Unity of Europe* (Washington, D.C.: Brookings Institution, 1963), pp. 10–11.

Martin Weil, *A Pretty Good Club* (New York: W. W. Norton, 1978), pp. 203–209, contains an extraordinarily simplistic account of the controversy between "Clayton's economists" and the Foreign Service, including a quite inaccurate reference to the plan I drafted in 1946.

2. Two participants at Yalta have judged Roosevelt's statement in somewhat different ways. Here is Churchill's paraphrase, from his *Triumph and Tragedy* (Boston: Houghton Mifflin, 1953), p. 353:

> At this first meeting Mr. Roosevelt had made a momentous statement. He had said that the United States would take all reasonable steps to preserve peace, but not at the expense of keeping a large army in Europe, three thousand miles away from home. The American occupation

would therefore be limited to two years. Formidable questions rose in my mind. If the Americans left Europe Britain would have to occupy single-handed the entire western portion of Germany. Such a task would be far beyond our strength.

In *Witness to History, 1929–1969* (New York: W. W. Norton, 1973), p. 184, Charles Bohlen challenged this interpretation on the grounds that Roosevelt was "talking in the context of a semi-permanent occupation of certain places in Germany by still united allies following a peace treaty." I rather doubt that Bohlen's assessment is adequate. After all, the American performance after World War I made U.S. staying power in the wake of World War II a central question for all parties interested in Europe's future. Churchill's judgment, in itself, made the statement "momentous." It is perhaps worth noting that the statement was so deeply etched in the Soviet records that Khrushchev referred to it in his conversation in Vienna with Kennedy in 1961 when challenging the legitimacy of NATO. See W. W. Rostow, *The Diffusion of Power* (New York: Macmillan, 1972), p. 226.

3.   The first account appeared in the column of Joseph and Stewart Alsop (*Washington Post*, April 24, 1946, p. 11). The following day, news reports were published by the Associated Press (John M. Hightower, *Washington Post*, p. 6) and the *New York Times* (Bertram D. Hulen), p. 3. See Appendix B.

4.   *Foreign Relations of the United States, 1946*, vol. 5, p. 554.

5.   Public opinion polls over the period 1945 to 1946 show that a substantial American majority was prepared to keep troops in Europe, Japan, and even China; that the rate and terms of discharge from the service were judged fair; that a rapid shift occurred toward reliance on U.S. strength rather than the U.N. for defense; that suspicion of Soviet intentions, never low, rapidly increased. On the other hand, most politicians took the view that the public clamor for demobilization was irresistible. For a discussion of the evidence for both views see Nancy Boardman, *Public Opinion and United States Foreign Policy, 1937–1956* (Cambridge, Mass.: Center for International Studies, M.I.T., undated [circa 1958]), pp. 49–62.

6. In 1930 the Republicans won both houses, but by an exceedingly narrow margin in the House of Representatives. The death of several members and subsequent by-elections shifted the balance to the Democrats—thus, the fifteen- rather than sixteen-year gap in Republican control of both houses.

7. George F. Kennan, *American Diplomacy, 1900–1950* (Chicago: University of Chicago Press, 1951), p. 120. The theme appears also, in positive form, in Kennan's equally celebrated long cable of February 22, 1946; see Barton J. Bernstein and Allen J. Matusow (eds.), *The Truman Administration: A Documentary History* (New York: Harper and Row, 1966), pp. 211–212.

8. Churchill, *Triumph and Tragedy*, p. 365. J. F. Byrnes, *Speaking Frankly* (New York: Harper and Brothers, 1947), p. 31, agrees that more time was spent at Yalta on Poland than any other subject. See also Bohlen, *Witness to History*, pp. 187–192, on the central role of the Polish question at Yalta.

9. J. Stalin, letter to Lenin of June 12, 1920, quoted in V. I. Lenin, *Collected Works*, 3d Russian ed. (Moscow, 1935), vol. 25, n. 141, p. 624.

10. Averell Harriman, *America and Russia in a Changing World* (Garden City: Doubleday, 1971), p. 44.

11. There is, literally, no reference of substance to U.S. policy toward Poland in Truman's *Memoirs* beyond Potsdam (vol. 1, p. 411). Much the same is true of Byrnes' *Speaking Frankly*, where the last reference to the Polish government is in the context of the debate in London in September 1945 over the Rumanian treaty (p. 101). The grim sequence from Yalta to the crudely fixed Polish election and the new constitution of February 1947 is traced out in detail in Edward J. Rozek, *Allied Wartime Diplomacy: A Pattern in Poland* (New York: John Wiley, 1958), pp. 338–437.

12. Lucius D. Clay, *Decision in Germany* (Garden City: Doubleday, 1950), pp. 121–122.

13. Dwight D. Eisenhower, *Crusade in Europe* (Garden City: Doubleday, 1948), p. 458.

14. For Clay's observations on the evolution of the U.S.-Soviet relationship and its limits, see *Decision in Germany*, pp. 107, 136–138, 159–162.

15. The passage that follows is based on conversations in Berlin with Clay, Robert Murphy, William Draper, and others in early June 1946. I was sent with J. K. Galbraith to negotiate with Clay a common American policy on Ruhr coal production to be urged on the British, within whose zone the Ruhr lay. The protracted character of our negotiations with Clay provided ample time to exchange views on other issues. Some, but not all, of the discussion is reflected in Appendix E.

16. Clay, *Decision in Germany*, p. 79. Clay persuaded Byrnes to retain the following sentence which the secretary considered eliminating from his speech: "As long as an occupation force is required in Germany, the Army of the United States will be a part of that occupation force."

17. Bohlen, *Witness to History*, pp. 175–177.

18. *Foreign Relations of the United States, 1946*, vol. 5, pp. 624–625, 628–629, 631–633. Among those pressing actively for German unity within EUR was David Harris, whose memorandum "Future Policy toward Germany" of March 26, 1946, is reproduced in Appendix H (740.00119 Control [Germany] 3-2646). Harris was not, however, a member of the Foreign Service.

19. Ibid., pp. 518–519.

20. Ibid., *1945*, vol. 3, p. 890 (November 3, 1945), p. 916, n. 8 (December 8, 1945); *1946*, vol. 5, pp. 505–507 (February 24, 1946), p. 509 (March 1, 1946).

21. Ibid., *1946*, vol. 5, p. 506.

22. Robert Murphy, *Diplomat among Warriors* (Garden City: Doubleday, 1964), p. 303. Before I left London in late April 1945, a senior American colleague and I were invited to lunch at a Pall Mall club with an RAF friend and a Foreign Office official whom we had never met. We were a bit surprised when it gradually emerged that the purpose of the exercise was for the Foreign Office official to suggest gently that we ought to begin thinking about an Anglo-American-led Western bloc to contain the Soviet Union in the postwar world.

23. *Foreign Relations of the United States, 1946*, vol. 6, p. 758.

24. From Bernstein and Matusow, *Truman Administration*, p. 245.

25. Clifford informs me that the report was printed in ten copies. In the morning of the day after he sent it to Truman, he was

called by the president on the telephone around 6:00 A.M. and asked how many copies existed and who had them. When informed that he alone had possession of the other copies, Truman ordered Clifford to bring them to the president's office early in the working day. Truman told Clifford that the document was explosive and must not be distributed. On being presented with the remaining copies, Truman counted them and locked them up. The document is now available at the Truman Library. The passages quoted from this report on pp. 46–50 above are extracted from pp. 72–79 of Clifford's text.

26. *Foreign Relations of the United States, 1947*, vol. 3, pp. 241–247.

27. These conversations can be traced in ibid., *1945*, vol. 3, pp. 897–912.

28. This reaction to the French proposals is explicitly reflected in the following concurring opinion of March 15, 1946, filed by ESP (the office containing GA), in an otherwise agreed working-level State Department paper urging that the Ruhr-Rhineland not be detached from Germany:

> ESP concurs with the recommendation that the French proposal for the separation of the Ruhr and Rhineland from Germany be rejected and with much of the underlying analysis of the supporting paper on which it has collaborated. It desires, however, to submit certain supplementary observations.
>
> *Analysis*
>
> The position taken in the subject paper is that this government should proceed with the *status quo*, making certain limited concessions to the French concept of their security requirements; and that should Europe split into exclusive eastern and western blocs, the boundary of the western bloc should be sought on the Elbe, rather than at the periphery of the Ruhr-Rhineland area. The paper does not address itself to the extent to which acceptance of central German administrative agencies would compromise the possibility of the latter outcome.
>
> ESP regards the description of the *status quo*, in the subject paper, as incomplete in relation to the underlying

French view. The French proposals arose in considerable part from the assumption that the United States interest and effective intervention in Europe would, as after 1918, prove to be transitory. From this assumption the French draw the conclusion that the long-run possibilities of a non-bloc structure for Europe, within the framework of Major Power accord, are remote.

It is appreciated that not only the French, by their proposal, but also the United Kingdom and the U.S.S.R. by their action, are conducting foreign policy in Europe on a similar assumption and a similar conclusion. In this they have been supported by the provisions of the Potsdam Agreement, which provided a truce with respect to Germany, but failed to set out a framework for Europe as a whole. Under these circumstances, a negative answer to the basic French proposals would appear to call for a fresh demonstration by the United States of its concern for and belief in the maintenance of one rather than two Europes.

There is further room for grave doubt whether the split of Europe at the Elbe, should continued quadripartite negotiation throughout Europe be impossible, would effectively serve the security interests of the United States or of Western Europe. Such a solution would involve the surrender by the West of its strong moral hold, if presently weak diplomatic leverage in Eastern Europe. It is, further, likely that such a solution would prove little more stable than the French scheme, and that the conception of security for the West it represents would prove almost equally illusory.

Recommendations

ESP favors the numbered recommendations of the subject paper and supports the position taken with respect to Alternative B.

ESP would further recommend for consideration, however, that the quadripartite negotiation of the French proposals for the separation of the Ruhr and the Rhineland from Germany be made the occasion for a major diplomatic offensive by the United States designed to halt and reverse the present movement towards an exclusive bloc structure in Europe. Out of its experience with a limited range of relevant issues, ESP has prepared a partial formulation for such an approach.

29. Eugene V. Rostow had served during the war as a State Department officer in North Africa in 1943 and subsequently as an assistant to Dean Acheson. After a long-delayed back operation, he returned as a professor to the Yale Law School. The cited conversation was on the telephone. His views on Germany and Europe were published in "The Partition of Germany and the Unity of Europe," *Virginia Quarterly Review* 23, no. 1 (Winter 1947): 18–33. He argues that European unity is the only method to prevent Germany from again disrupting the balance of power and that only an economically revived Germany partitioned into several component states could be safely absorbed in a unified Europe. The article also reflects anxiety that Byrnes' Stuttgart speech and concurrent Soviet verbal support for German unity signaled a competition for German nationalist sentiment of considerable danger.

30. During the 1960s, when I dealt with high officials of the Austrian government whose experience reached back to the immediate postwar days, I once asked why the Russians acquiesced in this arrangement. The judgment was that they believed the people of Austria would be so grateful for Soviet liberation that they would be pro-Communist. I am not sure that assessment is adequate, but I know of none better.

31. Jean Monnet, *Memoirs* (Garden City: Doubleday, 1978), pp. 249–255.

32. I recruited Frederick Nolting, trained as a lawyer, into GA while still in naval uniform, to help work on the tangled issues of German assets in Austria. He transferred, with our encouragement, to the Northern European section of EUR and ultimately rose to ambassadorial level. In a telephone conversation of February 29, 1980, he recalled the mood among his EUR colleagues in September 1946.

33. Bohlen, *Witness to History*, p. 257.

34. Dean Acheson, *Present at the Creation: My Years in the State Department* (New York: W. W. Norton, 1969), p. 265. George

Curry summarizes Byrnes' achievement in similar terms in *James F. Byrnes, 1945–47*, vol. 14 of *The American Secretaries of State and Their Diplomacy* (New York: Cooper Square Publishers, 1965), pp. 309–310: "It took the experience of repeated failures to reach agreement during the spring and summer of 1946, the realization that Eastern Europe was gone and that plans for the joint administration of Germany would not be honored, to convince Byrnes that the realities of the situation demanded more firmness than patience. . . . The period was one in which there was a gradual shift from a policy of cooperation with the Soviets to one approaching 'containment'. . ."

35. S. F. Bemis, *John Quincy Adams* (New York: Knopf, 1949), p. 364.

36. Letter from George Kennan to the author, probably in 1958. Neither Mr. Kennan's files nor mine proved capable of retrieving the exact date.

37. W. W. Rostow, *The American Diplomatic Revolution* (Oxford: Clarendon Press, 1946), especially pp. 24–25. I left the State Department in September 1946 to accept the post of Harmsworth Professor of American History for the year 1946 to 1947. An inaugural lecture is delivered any time a new professor is ready to hold forth. When I took up the visiting professorship at Oxford, I had contracted to go to Harvard as an associate professor of economic history. Harvard graciously granted me a year's leave of absence. In late June 1947, while I was honeymooning in Paris, Myrdal tracked me down and asked me to join him in helping set up the ECE in Geneva. He said that he understood I had a hand in the parentage of the institution, that it was coming to life at a difficult time, and he challenged me to back my play. My wife and I, after a visit to Geneva, decided to cast in our lot for a few years with the enterprise as a small personal contribution to the long future of Europe since, by the time we made our decision, Molotov had left Paris and it was clear the Marshall Plan would proceed on a Western basis. I resigned, therefore, from Harvard and worked in Geneva as special assistant to Myrdal from 1947 to 1949 and as a consultant in the summer of 1950. Thus, while my bureaucratic crusading in the State

Department in 1946 had only an extremely limited impact on the course of history, it had a considerable effect on my professional life.

38. The best available account of the creation of ECE is in Wightman, *Economic Co-operation in Europe*, pp. 3–25. See also W. W. Rostow, "The Economic Commission for Europe," *International Organization* 3 (1949): 254–268.

39. Porter has filed a set of papers in the Truman Library bearing on the period 1946 to 1947, including his perspective on the origins of the Marshall Plan. They are accompanied by a useful summary essay, "From Morgenthau Plan to Marshall Plan: A Memoir."

40. The documentary record shows that Byrnes' formal support for the ECE was obtained by November 14, 1946 (memorandum of telephone conversation between Willard Thorp, at the Council of Foreign Ministers meeting in New York, and L. D. Stinebower at the State Department). My memory is that Lubin had earlier gone from London to Paris to brief Byrnes on the institution being hatched in London; Byrnes expressed some surprise on that occasion that the idea still in his briefcase had emerged on the diplomatic scene but offered no objection to Lubin's proceeding with the enterprise.

41. See Václav Kostelecký, "The Birth of ECE," draft chapter 1 of the history of the ECE on which he is now at work. Mr. Kostelecký was good enough to make available to me this draft chapter.

42. In its early years, at least, the annual meetings of the commission itself were, indeed, marked by a good deal of polemics. The work of the technical committees, subcommittees, and panels was conducted quietly and in private with virtually no intrusion of political rhetoric.

43. Paul R. Porter's file on this period at the Truman Library contains six letters of mine written from Oxford in the winter and spring of 1947. Although I have no recollection of the matter, I apparently contributed to the drafting of some staff papers, including one for the March 1947 Moscow conference on Germany. Coming down to London, from time to time, I talked with Porter and his colleagues about the need—evident to all—for a more unified, better financed, long-range

European recovery effort. I had similar conversations with Oliver Franks, provost of The Queen's College, of which I was a fellow, and with some British officials. I cite these personal exchanges not because they were influential but to suggest that the sense that something big and new was required if Europe was to revive was in the air over the difficult winter of 1946–47. I also met in London with some old friends who had been on Marshall's staff in Moscow in the frustrating sessions on Germany and received in late April 1947 a firsthand report of their reaction, foreshadowing the Marshall Plan effort.

44. Ellen Clayton Garwood, *Will Clayton: A Short Biography* (Freeport, N.Y.: Books for Libraries Press, 1958), pp. 115–121.

45. Joseph M. Jones, *The Fifteen Weeks* (New York: Viking, 1955), p. 218.

46. George F. Kennan, *Memoirs, 1925–1950* (Boston: Little, Brown, 1967), pp. 325–326.

47. The most comprehensive older treatments of the Marshall Plan and its origins are Harry Bayard Price, *The Marshall Plan and Its Meaning* (Ithaca: Cornell University Press, 1955), and Jones, *Fifteen Weeks*. There are several important newer studies, including John Gimbel, *The Origins of the Marshall Plan* (Stanford: Stanford University Press, 1976), Ernst Van der Beugel, *From Marshall Aid to Atlantic Partnership* (Amsterdam: Elsevier Publishing Company, 1966), and Hadley Arkes, *Bureaucracy, the Marshall Plan and the National Interest* (Princeton: Princeton University Press, 1972). Two useful scholarly articles with differing interpretations are Thomas G. Paterson, "The Quest for Peace and Prosperity: International Trade, Communism and the Marshall Plan," in Barton J. Bernstein (ed.), *Politics and Policies of the Truman Administration* (Chicago: University of Chicago Press, 1970), and Scott Jackson, "Prologue to the Marshall Plan: The Origins of the American Commitment for a European Recovery Program," *Journal of American History* 65, no. 4 (March 1979): 1043–1068.

Two valuable accounts by participants regarding the events, personalities, and issues that influenced the formulation of the Marshall Plan are Acheson, *Present at the Creation*, and Kennan, *Memoirs*. Interesting but more narrowly focused accounts are Kindleberger, "Origins of the Marshall Plan," and Garwood's treatment of her father's role in *Will Clayton*.

Broader works on American foreign policy during the Cold War period often include valuable material on the origins of the Marshall Plan. Such accounts include Wightman, *Economic Co-operation in Europe*, Beloff, *The United States and the Unity of Europe*, Robert H. Ferrell, *George C. Marshall*, vol. 15 of *The American Secretaries of State and Their Diplomacy* (New York: Cooper Square Publishers, 1966), and Herbert Feis, *From Trust to Terror: The Onset of the Cold War, 1945–1950* (New York: W. W. Norton, 1970).

48. Joseph Jones traces in some detail the linkage between the work in 1946 within Clayton's staff, leading to the creation of the ECE, and the 1947 staff work on the Marshall Plan (*Fifteen Weeks*, pp. 240–244).

49. The relevant Planning Staff documents are found in *Foreign Relations of the United States, 1947*, vol. 3, pp. 220–229.

50. The documents referenced at the end of this note seem to support the following conclusions regarding American policy toward ECE at the time the Marshall Plan was formulated:

1. There is no evidence that the U.S. sabotaged or even deliberately abandoned ECE as a vehicle for implementing the Marshall Plan.

2. With the exception of Will Clayton, the other high-level officials in the State Department seemed to harbor ambivalent feelings about ECE.

a. If honest Soviet cooperation regarding a recovery program could be obtained, U.S. officials had no objection to placing the program under ECE jurisdiction, although the problems of implementation would be more complex.

b. Conversely, if it became clear that the U.S.S.R. would participate only for the purpose of internal sabotage, then it would be preferable if the Western European states formed a separate organization.

c. Clayton, probably as a result of his experience with the Soviets during ECE's first session in early May, had clearly abandoned any optimism concerning the use of the organization.

3. Throughout May and June, American officials stated repeatedly that it was up to the Europeans to decide whether to use ECE for the new recovery program.

4. Principal opposition to ECE during this period came from London and Paris, not Washington.

5. It was not until Molotov's performance at Paris that the U.S. urged other European governments to bypass the ECE.

See *Foreign Relations of the United States, 1947*, vol. 3, pp. 220–229, 235–237, 249–251, 263, 296, 309–310.

51. W. W. Rostow, *British Economy of the Nineteenth Century* (Oxford: Clarendon Press, 1948), p. 143.

52. Bohlen, *Witness to History*, p. 256.

53. A. H. Vandenberg, Jr. (ed.), *The Private Papers of Senator Vandenberg* (Boston: Houghton Mifflin, 1952), pp. 11, 134, 148.

54. Monnet, *Memoirs*, p. 109.

55. See, for example, the references to divided authority and multiple objectives of Soviet authorities in East Germany in Appendix E, pp. 142–144.

56. For an authoritative review of the facts and negotiations bearing on a postwar U.S. loan to the U.S.S.R. and a critical view of the revisionist literature on the subject, see E. V. Rostow, *Peace in the Balance* (New York: Simon and Schuster, 1972), pp. 108–133.

57. *Foreign Relations of the United States, Diplomatic Papers, the Conference at Malta and Yalta, 1945* (Washington D.C.: Government Printing Office, 1955), p. 977.

58. Vandenberg, *Private Papers of Senator Vandenberg*, p. 148.

59. See, for example, Kostelecký, "Birth of ECE," on Myrdal's discussions in Moscow at the time of the Marshall Plan offer. Indeed, as Acheson (quoting Ernest Bevin's account) indicates, Stalin's decision may have been finally made only during the Paris conference (*Present at the Creation*, p. 313):

"In two weeks' time they met with Molotov in Paris to discuss how Europeans might devise a European recovery plan, its requirements, and the parts they would play in it. The tripartite aspect of the talks soon blew up. I have described the scene as Bevin told it to me: "It seems that Molotov has a bump on his forehead which swells when he is under emotional strain. The matter was being debated and Molotov had raised relatively minor questions or objections at various points, when a telegram was handed to him. He turned pale and the bump on his forehead swelled. After that, his attitude changed and he became much more harsh. . . . I suspect that Molotov must have thought that the instruction sent him was stupid; in any case, the withdrawal of the Russians made operations much more simple."

On the next day, July 3, Bevin and Bidault issued a joint communiqué inviting twenty-two other European nations to send representatives to Paris to consider a recovery plan. (Czechoslovakia, which had at first agreed to attend, withdrew its acceptance after a visit to Moscow by Premier Gottwald and poor Jan Masaryk, the Foreign Secretary.) Once again General Marshall's judgment and his luck combined to produce the desired result.

60. Clay, *Decision in Germany*, pp. 123–124.
61. Patricia Dawson Ward, *The Threat to Peace: James Byrnes and the Council of Foreign Ministers, 1945–1946* (Kent, Ohio: Kent State University Press, 1979), p. 177.
62. Byrnes, *Speaking Frankly*, pp. 159–160.
63. For a brilliant rationale of the case for a split Europe, with Eastern Europe under Soviet hegemony, see A. W. De Porte, *Europe between the Superpowers: The Enduring Balance* (New Haven: Yale University Press, 1979).
64. Although "traditionalist" and "revisionist" treatments of the early Cold War disagree on numerous issues, they generally share a common deficiency. With rare exceptions, they devote insufficient attention to the events and processes taking place during the crucial year 1946.

Traditionalist interpretations such as John Spanier, *American Foreign Policy since World War II* (New York: Frederick

A. Praeger, 1960), Adam Ulam, *The Rivals: America and Russia since World War II* (New York: Viking, 1971), and Feis, *From Trust to Terror*, argue that the Cold War resulted from an essential, if somewhat belated, American response to postwar Soviet expansionism which had already claimed Eastern Europe and threatened to engulf the remainder of the continent. Historians adopting that thesis focus on the waning Soviet-American cooperation during the final months of World War II and then proceed to analyze the cornerstones of America's official Cold War policy in 1947, the Truman Doctrine and the Marshall Plan. With the exception of the Iranian crisis, Spanier largely ignores the crucial period from early 1946 until the promulgation of the Truman Doctrine in March of the following year. Ulam and Feis pay more attention to the events of that period, especially Byrnes' treaty negotiations and the dispute concerning German reparations, but both writers exhibit an urgency to move on to the supposedly more interesting and significant developments in 1947. Neither scholar, for instance, examines the creation of the Economic Commission for Europe.

Revisionist authors such as Walter LaFeber, *America, Russia and the Cold War, 1945–1971* (New York: John Wiley and Sons, 1972), Stephen Ambrose, *Rise to Globalism: American Foreign Policy since 1938* (Baltimore: Penguin, 1971), Lloyd Gardner, *Architects of Illusion: Men and Ideas in American Foreign Policy, 1941–1949* (Chicago: Quadrangle, 1970), William Appleman Williams, *The Tragedy of American Diplomacy* (Cleveland: World Publishing, 1959), Gabriel Kolko and Joyce Kolko, *The Limits of Power: The World and United States Foreign Policy, 1945–1954* (New York: Harper and Row, 1972), and Thomas Paterson, *Soviet-American Confrontation* (Baltimore: Johns Hopkins University Press, 1973), likewise concentrate on events in 1945 and 1947 far more than the intervening period. According to most revisionist historians, the Cold War emerged primarily because of American efforts to establish a global economic order based upon the "open door" principle. Since all regions of the world were to remain available to American trade and investment, it was essential to stimulate the creation of capitalist regimes friendly to the United States. When the Soviet Union resisted such intrusion into Eastern Europe, an area essential to Russian security interests, the United States responded with economic coercion and President Truman displayed a degree of personal truculence that ruptured any chance for continued American-Soviet cooperation.

A somewhat different view is expressed by John Lewis Gaddis in *The United States and the Origins of the Cold War, 1941–1947* (New York: Columbia University Press, 1972). Gaddis shares many of the revisionist assumptions, but he seems less concerned than most revisionists or traditionalists in assessing "blame" for the onset of the Cold War. Instead, he views the conflict more as an inevitable dispute arising from differing Soviet and American world views.

Revisionist authors assume the Cold War was already an established fact by late 1945 or early 1946. Walter LaFeber effectively summarizes this thesis when he asserts that Stalin's speech in February 1946 and Churchill's "Iron Curtain" address the following month represented joint declarations of Cold War. The Truman Doctrine and the Marshall Plan, therefore, were little more than a shift in America's already operational Cold War strategy.

Like their traditionalist brethren, revisionist authors treat 1946 rather superficially. Gaddis, Paterson, and the Kolkos examine that period in greater detail than most other scholars, but even their treatments are not sufficiently comprehensive. None of the revisionist accounts mentions the Acheson-Clayton plan, and only Paterson and the Kolkos analyze the creation of the Economic Commission for Europe and its significance.

Both the traditionalist and revisionist factions are inhibited in dealing with 1946 by their implicit assumption that either the Soviet Union or the United States pursued a predetermined, deliberate, sophisticated strategy to achieve postwar global domination. Greater attention to events in 1946 might have suggested a different thesis—that the ultimate Cold War confrontation between the two powers resulted less from any firm conscious design on either side than it did from incremental increases in tension caused by individual episodes of miscalculation and misunderstanding, flowing, of course, from differing presuppositions but not from firmly fixed purposes.

Index

⟨

party, 83; and division of Europe, 81, 196n; and Donovan, 10; and European unity, 151; and Foreign Service, 58; and Marshall Plan, 81, 83; meeting with Molotov, 1945, 16; and Poland, 16, 18, 184n; price controls of, 11; and Roosevelt, 82; and Stalin, 47, 84; and Truman Doctrine, 81; USSR, policy toward, 47; and Wallace, 46
Truman Doctrine, 50, 73, 81, 84, 92, 195n–196n
Truman Library, 81, 186n, 190n
Turkey, 98; and US, 73; and USSR, 13–14, 73, 83, 157

Ulam, Adam, 195n
Ulbricht, Walter, 168, 171
Ukraine, technical commission, proposed membership in, 114; UN, regional European organization, proposed membership in, 96; USSR, 13
Union of Soviet Socialist Republics (USSR), and Acheson-Clayton proposal, 84; and All-European settlement, 75, 105, 107, 122, 163; Allies, relations with, 41; and Austria, 15, 55, 60, 98, 188n; and Bulgaria, 99; and Byrnes, 89–90; Council for Europe proposal, 113; and Czechoslovakia, 99; and division of Europe, 5, 8–9, 27, 41, 45–46, 58–60, 62, 77, 87, 90–91, 98–99, 101–104, 120, 122, 127–128, 187n; and ECE, 72–73, 192n–193n; ECITO, participation in, 54; and Estonia, 156; and Europe, Central, 14, 21, 104, 137; and Europe, Eastern, 7, 12–18, 41, 43, 45, 56, 58, 61, 68, 85–87, 89, 91, 95, 99, 104, 108–109, 121, 128, 137, 147, 194n–196n; and Europe, South-

eastern, 95, 128; and European unity, 87, 99–100, 128, 154, 163; expansion into a major world power, 41, 86, 95, 104, 135, 155, 157–160, 164; and Finland, 13, 99; foreign policy of, in Europe, 6, 12–24, 27, 56, 59, 61, 92–93, 98–99, 102–104, 137; and France, 44, 54; and German Communism, 167–174; and German disarmament, 131–132; and German reparations, 19, 43, 125–127, 144; and Germany, 7, 18, 27, 29, 43–44, 55, 58, 68, 87–88, 105, 117, 125–126, 128, 130–133, 142–143, 155–156, 167–179, 188n; and Hungary, 13, 99; and Iran, 13–14, 85; and Kennan, 42, 85, 134–137; and Korea, 92; and Latvia, 156; and Lithuania, 156; and Marshall, 73–74, 90, 92, 191n; and Marshall Plan, 74, 85, 87, 92; and Middle Eastern oil, 98; military security of, 105, 108, 134–135; nationalism of, 134–135, 156–157, 159; and Poland, 12–18, 45, 84, 156; and Potsdam, 6, 103, 127–130, 132, 143; propaganda of, 136, 159; and Ruhr-Rhineland, 133, 187n; and Rumania, 156; seizure of equipment, 19, 127, 132, 143, 172; and technical commissions, proposed for Europe, 114, 121; and Turkey, 13–14, 73, 83; and UK, 146, 156; UN, proposed regional European organization, 96, 109–110; as unified market, 78; and US, assumption of US withdrawal from Europe, 56–57; and US, economic aid from, 70, 104, 193n; and US, Foreign Service view of, 67, 121; and US, military security of, 48; and US, possible misreading of inten-

210

tions, 196n–197n; and US, test
of USSR intentions, 68, 80, 93;
as wartime ally, 39; Western
contacts of, 143
United Nations, 83, 109, 110, 112,
116, 151, 153, 158, 183n; and
Acheson-Clayton proposal,
94–101; Assembly of, 96, 99,
109; and Austria, 98; and Bohlen, 41; and division of Europe,
59, 61–62, 94–99, 105–106;
ECE, 70–73, 75, 96–99, 189n–
190n, 193n, 195n–196n; Economic and Social Council
(ECOSOC) of, 70–72, 96, 112,
116, 119, 123, 125; European regional structure, proposed, 5,
62, 96–101, 106–110, 112–113,
121–125, 151–154; Relief and
Rehabilitation Administration
(UNRRA) of, 70–71, 104, 107; Security Council of, 96, 99, 109,
113, 121
United States, and All-European settlement, 75, 94–119, 163, 187n;
and Austria, 60; and balance of
power, 86; and coal, 54, 138–
148; and Cold War, 92, 196n–
197n; and Council for Europe
proposal, 113; Czechoslovakian-
Americans, 41; democratic
countries, economic aid to,
48–49, 102; diplomatic traditions of, 62–67; and division of
Europe, 3–9, 22–23, 26–27,
29, 38–50, 57–58, 60, 64,
68–69, 75, 87, 91, 94–119, 122,
126–134, 150, 181n, 187n; domestic economic and political
life of, postwar, 10–12, 134–
137; ECE, support for, 72, 192n–
193n; Europe, Eastern, 85, 89,
102–103; Europe, Eastern, economic aid to, 70, 98, 103–104;
Europe, economic aid to, 4–5,
34, 56, 70, 77, 102–104, 118,

155, 162; and European nationalism, 78–79; and European
security, 137; and European
unity, 110, 132, 154, 163; and
First World War, 64; and France,
44, 53–54, 70, 144, 147, 181n,
187n; and German reparations,
19–23, 102, 127–130, 132–133;
and Germany, 26–28, 40, 44,
52, 89–90, 102, 105, 162, 164–
179, 185n; and Greece, 73; and
Korea, 92; and Latin America,
159; military security of, 48–49,
157, 187n; occupation of Germany, 26, 138–148, 165–167,
171, 182n; and Poland, 12–13,
15–16, 18, 27, 81, 85; Polish-
Americans, 41; presence in postwar Europe, military and political, 5, 43, 55, 57, 87, 91–92, 95,
162, 182n–183n, 185n; and Turkey, 73; and UK, 66, 70, 77, 89,
138–148; UN, involvement in,
41; UN, proposed regional European organization, 96, 110, 112;
as unified market, 78; USSR, economic aid to, 70, 109, 193n; and
USSR, expansion of, 48–50, 59,
92–93, 99, 155–164, 195n;
USSR, possible misreading of intentions, 196n–197n; USSR,
public opinion in US toward, 12,
49, 83–84, 136, 157–158, 183n;
USSR, US test of intentions of,
68; Western bloc, support for, 6,
99, 101, 103, 134, 147
US-USSR relations, 14–15, 18, 20,
24–27, 41, 43, 46–50, 59,
61–62, 68, 80–81, 83–84, 89,
92–93, 98–99, 103–104, 122,
126–138, 142–144, 146–147,
156–157, 159–160, 164, 184n,
189n, 195n–196n

Vandenberg, A. H., Jr., 193n
Vandenberg, Arthur H., 28; and

DATE DUE

JAN 27 '84			
FE 2 84			
FEB 2 8 '85			
GAYLORD			PRINTED IN U.S.A.